NURSE

past, present and future

THE MAKING OF MODERN NURSING

EDITED BY KATE TRANT AND SUSAN USHER

black dog
publishing
london uk

Introduction

2010 marks 100 years since the death of Florence Nightingale. It is an opportunity to celebrate the contribution nurses have made to the welfare of populations around the globe. It is also an occasion to look back on some of the key developments in nursing since Nightingale to see how the profession is redefining itself for the twenty-first century. Nurses today are at the heart of efforts to care for ageing populations, increase health equity around the globe, prevent the chronic diseases that risk crippling health systems, all the while providing the ever more sophisticated care made possible by rapid developments in science and technology. How is the profession evolving to meet this very tall order?

Our work on the periphery of health systems, in hospital design and health policy, has led us into some of the current debates underway within nursing. We see the expectations our societies have for nurses to help meet current challenges, and we see the barriers that prevent us from benefiting fully from their expertise. We encounter nurses who are making a tremendous difference to the profession, the health system and of course, to the patients they care for. A desire to capture and share the stories of personal, professional and social commitment to improving the lives of others is what prompted us to undertake this book.

We started talking to some of the nurses close at hand about their professional challenges and accomplishments. They referred us to other nurses, who referred us to other nurses, until we were talking to a Brazilian nurse about new methods of care for premature babies, a Japanese nurse about collaborative care following the earthquake in Kobe, Japan, and so many others. Nurses are generous with their time, and they have a lot to say.

We also approached global academic leaders to write about issues of central concern to nursing today: professionalisation, migration, education and interprofessional collaboration. Their work is at the forefront of nursing research that is redefining the profession. The discussions taking place within nursing address specific concerns in different countries, but focus on some overarching challenges: attracting and retaining sufficient numbers, assuring appropriate education, designing productive workplaces, redefining scopes of practice to enable nurses to assume new roles, forging more collaborative working relationships with other health professions, and assuming a stronger voice in the design of healthcare systems and social policy.

In much the same way as nursing itself, the book combines the academic and the practical. Each chapter takes on one aspect of nursing, combining research essays with personal accounts to illustrate how the progress of nursing has played out on the ground. Chapter 1 delves into how nursing identity has evolved in the past century, through changes in nursing education, designation and role. Chapter 2 broaches the issue of nurse migration from both global and personal perspectives. Chapter 3 looks at the various environments that constitute the nurse's workplace, from the hospital to the home to the field tent. And Chapter 4 traces the important role nurses have played in transforming care to improve the health of populations. Efforts today focus on promoting teamwork among healthcare providers, empowering patients to play a greater role in their health and well-being and ensuring that the dignity of patients—and nurses—is respected in the provision of care.

Which brings us back to Florence Nightingale. Although we are mindful that there are other nurse reformers who have influenced the direction and spirit of nursing, the legacy of Florence Nightingale is powerful and tenacious. As practices and attitudes to nursing have changed through the decades, her quiet influence has remained fundamental to what nurses do today. So many of the nurses we spoke to told us that, whatever changes in social, cultural and technological context we may have witnessed, the core values of care, compassion, dignity and common sense remain consistent. The newly refurbished Florence Nightingale Museum at St Thomas' Hospital in London is a celebration of her influence, and at the heart of the way that her legacy is communicated throughout the world.

We want to thank everyone who contributed their stories, essays and images to the book, along with the individuals who guided us through this project.

It is our hope that nurses reading the book draw inspiration from the experiences described by colleagues around the globe, that those outside the profession gain a better understanding of what nursing work entails and how it can be supported, and that young men and women deciding what to do with their lives come to see nursing as a profession through which they can truly change the world for the better.

Kate Trant, London
Susan Usher, Montréal

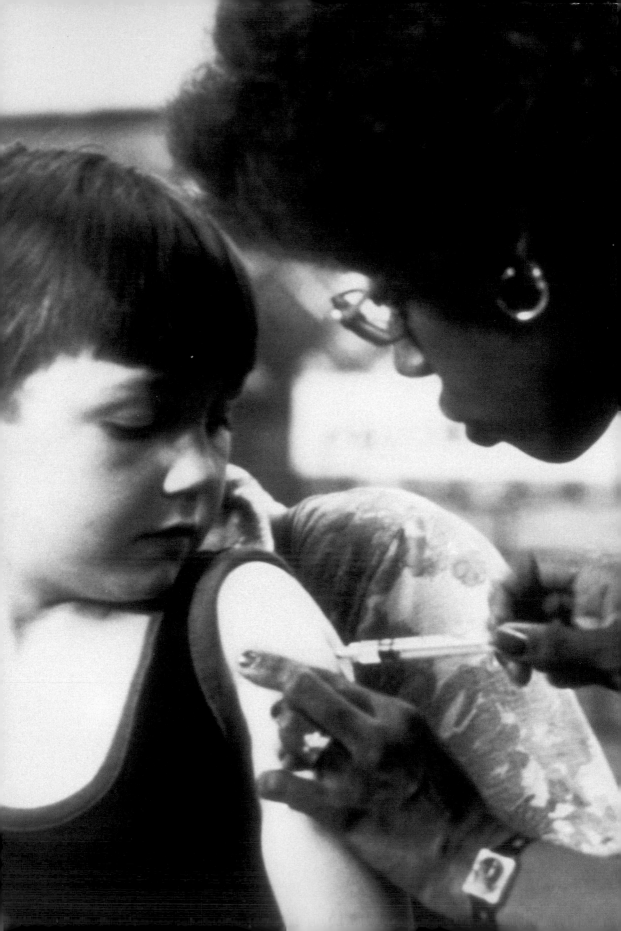

1

What is a Nurse?

What is a Nurse?

The millions of nurses who care for our populations come from every possible background and work in every imaginable setting. Education, social standing, and specific skills differ from place to place and over time. But nurses everywhere share an underlying drive to help people through difficult periods in life and it is this drive that truly defines nursing. When asked where it came from, most will refer back to a nurse they encountered at some point in their early lives who inspired them to acquire the knowledge that would enable them, in turn, to provide meaningful help. We might ask, as we look at past and present nurse identities, what children today might see that will inspire them to take up the challenge.

In this Chapter, Helen Sweet from the Wellcome Unit for the History of Medicine at the University of Oxford traces how and why the role of the nurse has evolved in the 100 years since Florence Nightingale's death. Eamonn Sullivan from Guys and St Thomas' Hospital then describes why Nightingale remains so relevant today. Changes in education and designation have had a profound effect on nurse identity. Helen Mussallem looks back at efforts she led in the 1960s to move nurse education out of hospitals in Canada, and Andrea Baumann from McMaster University provides a global view on nurse education today. To see what some of these changes have meant for individual nurses, we talked to Kelly Knoll about the trajectory that led to her becoming a nurse practitioner, a role that is pushing the boundaries of traditional nursing identity, and to Zena Edmund-Charles on the ways in which uniforms and propriety helped to define generations of nurses.

PREVIOUS PAGES Nurse vaccinating a child, Massachusetts, USA.

Community nurse in Essex, England, 2007.

Nurse at a patient's bedside, Canada, 2010.

The Evolution of Professional Nursing

Dr Helen Sweet, Wellcome Unit for the History of Medicine, University of Oxford, traces how nursing has evolved over the past century.

In Britain, nursing as a profession emerged from a heterogeneous background of care providers. These included self-employed independent practitioners or husband and wife 'teams', who sometimes intruded upon the sphere of the local surgeon or medical practitioner, and care-givers from religious sisterhoods. Other early nurses worked under contract to the voluntary hospitals and poor law relief committees.[1] Some combination of most of these care-givers would have been common across much of Europe in the early nineteenth century. While other developments played an important role in the gradual professionalisation of nursing, Florence Nightingale's ideas on sanitary reform and nurse education were essentially what propelled reforms to nursing in Britain after 1840. Her influence spread throughout the British Commonwealth and beyond.[2]

> She is a 'ministering angel' without any exaggeration in these hospitals, and as her slender form glides quietly along each corridor every poor fellow's face softens with gratitude at the sight of her. When all the medical officers have retired for the night, and silence and darkness have settled down upon these miles of prostrate sick, she may be observed alone, with a little lamp in her hand, making her solitary rounds.

The Times, Thursday 8 February 1855.

The end of World War One is often seen as marking a watershed between nursing as a vocation, where the 'character' and underlying altruistic ethos of the nurse was at least as important as her practical ability and knowledge, to a post-Nightingale era, in which uniformity of standards both in training and professional practice would prevail. But when we look beyond that important period in the evolution of nursing institutions, what appears is not a clear demarcation between one era and the next, but an evolutionary process that is still ongoing almost a century later as we continue to search for the ideal mode of training and as demands on the nursing profession continue to change.

Florence Nightingale, Scutari Hospital, 'An Angel of Mercy', engraved by Tomkins, 1855.

The Nightingale Pledge. Composed by a committee chaired by Lystra Gretter, an instructor of nursing at the Harper Hospital in Detroit, Michigan, The Nightingale Pledge was first used in 1893. It is an adaptation of the Hippocratic Oath taken by physicians. Now around 120 years old, many institutions have modified or dropped the pledge.

+ I solemnly pledge myself before God, and in the presence of this assembly, to pass my life in purity and to practice my profession faithfully.

+ I will abstain from whatever is deleterious and mischievous, and will not take or knowingly administer any harmful drug.

+ I will do all in my power to maintain and elevate the standard of my profession, and will hold in confidence all personal matters committed to my keeping and all family affairs coming to my knowledge in the practice of my calling.

+ With loyalty will I endeavor to aid the physician, in his work, and devote myself to the welfare of those committed to my care.

District Nurses attending to an injured girl, hop gardens, Herefordshire, England, 1940s.

Professionalisation

Following a protracted battle between powerful groups of pro- and anti- registrationists in Britain, nursing gradually emerged as a nationally regulated profession at the end of the 1920s, moving away from its nineteenth century status as a vocational occupation.[3] This transformation was confirmed both by the foundation of the Royal College of Nursing in 1916 and by the introduction of national regulation through legislation three years later (the Nurses Registration Act, 1919) and the subsequent formation of the General Nursing Council (GNC).[4] This change came earlier in other countries—in particular, South Africa, 1891, and New Zealand, 1901.[5] In the United States (US) the first Registration Act for Nurses was passed in 1903.[6] Australia followed the British lead and consequently only introduced registration in the early 1920s.[7]

The impact of a major, worldwide recession in the mid- to late 1920s and early 1930s impacted on pay and conditions of service generally, as infectious diseases and diseases associated with malnutrition became more common. This increased the nurse's workload, particularly in community nursing. The long hours and low pay, combined with an underlying view of nursing as a vocational service for unmarried women, combined to hamper recruitment.[8] Shortages of nurses persisted globally throughout the inter-war years and well into the second half of the twentieth century. These shortages were felt particularly in the maternity hospitals, hospitals for the elderly and chronically ill and in mental institutions. In the post-war era, an increase in nurse migration to developed countries increased this problem for less developed African and Asian countries that were struggling to train sufficient nurses to staff their own hospitals. Once trained, these nurses were often enticed abroad to work in hospitals in the UK, Europe, Canada and the US.

Nurses learning about the National Health Service structure in England, 1950.

The Changing Role of the Nurse

Fairly uniformly across the globe, the nurse's role evolved over the course of the twentieth century, from a largely domestic role to one that was highly technical and required specialised training. And as the role evolved, so did the direction taken by professionalisation, training and qualification, specialisation and even recruitment. The change was heavily influenced by societal changes, innovations in medicine, pharmacology, equipment and materials, and advances in transport and communication.

Changing health and welfare provisions had an important impact on the nursing profession. In the UK these included Acts of Parliament such as Maternity and Child Welfare legislation as well as Local Government Acts and a series of Education Acts from the late nineteenth century onwards.[9] Local government legislation, (poor law reform bills) impacted on hospital and public health administration and eventually made local government accountable for paying for some of the duties carried out by community nurses. This raised the profile of their public health role, while the Education Acts had an impact both on the health of patients and on the education of women who might be recruited into nursing.[10]

The introduction of the National Health Service (NHS) in the UK in 1948, followed closely by the Nurses Act of 1949, marked the beginning of a period of intense restructuring and reorganisation.[11] From this time on, nurses were no longer paid by local lay-run district nursing committees but came under the auspices of the NHS, with their pay and conditions now arbitrated through the civil service administration (Whitley Council). Efforts to raise the educational qualification requirements for recruits proved futile in Britain for many years, as nursing shortages became increasingly problematic and the apprenticeship system of training remained in place. Elsewhere in the world, university-based nurse training was being considered or established.[12]

Nursing students in a class at St Louis Children's Hospital, Missouri, USA, 1949.

Advances in Medicine and Pharmacology

Changes taking place in the professions of medicine and pharmacology would have an important impact on the evolution of nursing in the twentieth century. Medicine developed into a strong, male-dominated profession, hospital-based medicine rose to the fore and, with the improvements in anaesthetics and techniques, surgery became increasingly sophisticated as the century progressed. Nursing had to incorporate surgical techniques and procedures including operating theatre and anaesthetic nursing and post-operative wound care. As the surgery became more complex and specialised, venturing into burns and plastic surgery, thoracic, cardiovascular and neurosurgery, increasingly specialised nursing training and care became necessary.

This interdependent relationship between medicine and nursing produced a hierarchical shift within nursing: the more sophisticated the technology involved in a nursing specialty, the higher its perceived status became.[13] Nursing specialties such as intensive care gained respect, while others such as community, geriatric and psychiatric nursing were somewhat neglected. Nursing education mirrored this schism with the introduction first of the State Enrolled Nurse as a lower-tier nurse in the UK, Australia and New Zealand in the 1940s.[14] An upper tier was then created when degree and post-graduate university-based courses were instituted in the 1960s and 70s.

Elizabeth O'Connell, a graduate of the University of Washington School of Nursing, Washington, USA, late 1940s.

A study session for nursing students at the University of Washington School of Nursing, Washington, USA, 1959.

A Queen's Nurse visiting patients by car, Loch Fyne, Argyll, Scotland, 1959.

A nurse writing on the slate at the nurses' home so that visitors know where she is and can contact her in case of emergency, England, 1949.

Medication, Vaccination and Surgery

A wide range of new medicines became available as the twentieth century progressed, making it possible to treat a wide array of medical disorders. Sulphonamides and antibiotics could treat tuberculosis and numerous infections, insulin managed diabetes and better drugs were developed for cardiovascular disorders, psychological illnesses, epilepsy, strokes, etc. Although most of these were prescribed by doctors (until recent nurse-prescribing changed even this), the nurse's role and sphere of expertise had to expand to incorporate knowledge of their use and practicalities of their administration. New drugs also had a significant impact on nursing specialisation. For example, the introduction of antibiotics together with immunisation programmes was a major factor in the decline of Fever Nursing.[15] The emergence of sulphonamides and then antibiotics by mid-century, as well as vaccination, saw tuberculosis wards close as treatments changed. Patients could be nursed safely at home, and the disease all but disappeared.

Surgical nursing became more complex as anaesthetics and analgesics improved and post-operative infections were reduced by antibiotic cover. Nurses needed to develop skills not only in different kinds of surgical care, but in caring for critically ill patients. By the 1970s, nurse 'specialling' areas on surgical and medical wards gave way to intensive therapy units, renal units, high dependency wards and cardiac care units.[16] Likewise, the arrival of cytotoxic drugs and more effective treatments for cancer created demand for specialised oncology nurses. Improvements in pain control prompted the development of palliative care nursing as a specialty.

Community Nursing

In the community, district nursing also experienced a complete transformation. In rural areas in particular, travel by bicycle or even horseback at the beginning of the twentieth century was superseded by the scooter or motorbike by the 1920s and 30s. Post-war, the automobile enabled nurses to cover a larger geographic area and assume a heavier patient load.[17] The District Nurse was increasingly becoming a member of a primary care team, and by the 1960s was likely to work in an office, rather than working from home.[18] As part of this transition, dual and triple-duty roles, which combined nursing with midwifery and sometimes also health visiting, all but disappeared. In addition, a number of specialist groups of nurses emerged, including school nurses, community psychiatric nurses, stoma care nurses and a range of palliative care nurses. According to demand and healthcare system, variations of this range of community nursing have evolved across Europe, the US and Canada, Australia and sub-Saharan Africa.

Materials and Technologies

Germ theory and asepsis were incorporated into nursing technique by the end of the nineteenth century. The materials and instruments used for dressings and sterilisation, as well as the techniques used in their application, presented significant challenges to nurses' clinical practice. Initially, sterilisation was somewhat makeshift and nurses used a variety of methods involving disinfectants or heat. Night nurses would spend much of their shift packing drums with bandages, wool and gauze to be baked or autoclaved. Community nurses had to improvise using biscuit tins in ovens and boiling their instruments at patients' homes.

District Nurses leaving for work from their nurse's home, London, England, 1950s.

In the late 1960s, the advent of Central Sterilising Supply Departments (CSSDs), where sterilisation was done by non-nurses on a production line system, represented a major change and removed one more 'domestic' element from the nurse's role.

Pre-packed instruments, dressings, syringes and needles, and specialised pre-prepared dressing and surgical packs and solutions not only contributed to changes in clinical nursing methods and standards of practice, but also to nursing's professional image.

A Fluid Concept

Internationally, over the past 150 years, nursing has evolved at different rates and with different emphases, despite the early foundation of the International Council of Nurses in 1899, the first global organisation for nurses. As a country's health and welfare services developed to take advantage of advances in science and medicine, trained nurses were inevitably required in increasing numbers to staff these services.

The physical setting of care changed repeatedly during the twentieth century. At the end of the nineteenth century, community care was at its height and hospitalisation was not generally a first choice, particularly for the wealthy who preferred to hire a 'private' nurse and receive private medical care in their homes. As the century progressed and hospital-based specialties developed, this trend was reversed and hospitals were recognised as the place of choice for 'modern' medical, surgical and nursing care. Yet by the end of the century, shorter hospital stays and a move away from institutionalisation, together with a greater emphasis on health and wellbeing, had revived the need for a broad spectrum of 'care in the community' and the trend appears to have gone into reverse. In countries where much of the population live in rural areas with limited access to hospitals, this is a particularly important concept which has become a matter of urgent political concern. For example, in post-apartheid South Africa where much of the black African population was for years deprived of adequate nursing and medical care, the emphasis of government health policy since 1997 has moved firmly towards financing better primary healthcare.[19]

The evolution of the nurse's role has reflected changes in medicine and society. Today's modern degree-qualified, specialist nurse is trained to care for a rapid turnover of both acute and chronically ill patients in hospital. Community nurses must now be prepared to care for patients discharged just one or two days post-operatively, sometimes with intravenous infusions, drains and catheters, sutures, etc. Less qualified 'carers' now carry out many of tasks that would have fallen to the community nurse in previous decades.

As we look back across the twentieth century, and ahead into our current century, it becomes clear that the definition of what is a nurse can clearly only truly be understood as a fluid concept.

Before carrying out smallpox vaccinations, this public health nurse gives a lecture on the disease to schoolchildren, Vietnam.

A group of women and children at a housing project mobile clinic waiting for and receiving vaccinations, USA, 1972.

Why Florence Nightingale is Still Relevant to Us Today

Eamonn Sullivan, RN, came to the UK from Ireland to train as a nurse and is now Head of Performance for Quality and Nursing Standards at Guy's and St Thomas' Hospital, London. From the home of an early Nightingale ward, he looks at why Florence Nightingale continues to exert such a strong influence on nursing practice.

The essence of nursing has not changed in 150 years. Nursing is about care, compassion and dignity, advocacy, and good common sense; this remains unchanged despite changes in technology. Although the language would be different, the observations of Florence Nightingale's *Notes on Nursing* would still ring true if you were to read them in a modern book about nursing practice. Florence Nightingale's teachings and her moral direction remain critically important.

The principles of her care will probably stay the same forever. They are timeless. When we lose sight of these, that is where we come unstuck. Nursing is a very practical job. That is the bottom line; it is a 'roll your sleeves up and get stuck in' job, within a caring, compassionate and dignified framework. Our core job is looking after our patients and doing absolutely anything for them that they are unable to do for themselves. On the other hand, it is absolutely critical to have nurses who are trained to the highest academic standards, who can study and lead research at the highest level, and who can translate that into evidenced based nursing practice. It is a fine balance. The profession will wither if we do not have the ability to develop our own evidence base to drive forward research and education. But this should never be at the expense of the essence of nursing. It is a big challenge for nursing.

I believe that it is possible to over-theorise nursing. We need intelligent and articulate professionals, but really nursing is about caring and common sense. We are motivated by caring. In my opinion, a task-orientated structure that is combined with the individual nurse's intelligence, ability to think critically and in some cases work autonomously can produce good outcomes. There are things that have to be done—patients must be weighed, their charts must be filled in correctly, nutrition must be a priority and so on, but nursing is much more than these essential tasks. These are important opportunities for building the nurse-patient relationship, trust and empathy—the real art of nursing.

Florence Nightingale remains such a positive role model because of her leadership, and the way she achieved massive change. Her influence on healthcare was global. Although she was popular in her time, she was also unpopular with a lot of people but, despite the criticism, she always remained focused on the essence of care. Her objective was better patient care, and building an education system that would achieve this. Her discipline and organisational skills mean that she still epitomises the nurse leader who coordinates the hospital and keeps everything going; I find her inspirational for this.

Leadership and role models are crucial. For me, ward sisters are the most important people in the Health Service. They are the people who determine success or failure in terms of patient safety, patient experience and efficient care.

You can have the best surgeons, doing the most cutting-edge or life-saving surgery, but if the ward nursing team is not well-led or motivated, it will fall apart. Patients will get infections, they will fall out of bed, they will not receive the nutrition they need. The ward sister is pivotal—get that right and most other elements will fall into place.

Nurse training is very general and student nurses are exposed to a lot of different

MISS FLORENCE NIGHTINGALE.　　　L.S.Cᵒ.Nᵒ123.

Florence Nightingale, c 1860.

A ward in the hospital at Scutari, engraved by E Walker, 1856.

specialties. But it is the people who you are exposed to, your role models, who influence your decisions, as well as your own aptitudes and ambitions. There are great opportunities to move about within the system, certainly at the junior levels. Often people will then select the team that they really liked working with, and the nurses in any hospital will know the best wards to work on. That is down to the best leaders, the ward sisters who have fostered and grown the best teams.

I first encountered Nightingale when, as part of my first year training, we came to visit the Florence Nightingale Museum at St Thomas' Hospital. A significant strand of my training was the history of nursing and, though it did not influence me much then—as a student nurse, you are focusing on all the fancy skills and getting out and about—I began to appreciate the significance of what she did a year or so after becoming a staff nurse. I was also impressed by Mary Seacole. She had a very different role in the Crimea to Nightingale, and I believe she had even greater challenges because she was not white. For Mary Seacole to achieve what she achieved back in those days, as Nightingale did, is amazing.

I came to work at St Thomas' in 1994. The brand of the hospital was and is still strong. The Nightingale nurse, the Nightingale ward— all that is very powerful in a positive way and made a big impression on me. I did not choose to come here because of Florence Nightingale, I came because of the quality of the hospital. But that quality is, in part, a consequence of what she achieved.

I was very interested in her attitude to infection and discipline, and to the environment and its impact on wellbeing. Before Nightingale, there was no empirical evidence to support this, but now there is evidence to underpin her vision and her ideas in terms of wellbeing. Today those ideas seem simple but, at the time, they were completely pioneering.

As a military nurse in Iraq and Afghanistan, her experience in the Crimea really rings true for me. She had a strategic vision that other people simply did not have, and that so many women at that time were not allowed to have. She was light years ahead. Look at what she achieved at the field hospital. Yes, the conditions were primitive in comparison to today's care, but actually it was way ahead of anything that was being done anywhere else in the world;

Medicine chest used by Florence Nightingale during the Crimean War, 1854–1856, one of the central exhibits at the newly-refurbished Florence Nightingale Museum in London.

it was truly an enlightening period for military medical care. Even though we think of the Crimea as being brutal and awful, the standard of care that the soldiers received in the Crimea was better than ever before and there are many similarities to modern military healthcare. The care that soldiers receive in Iraq and Afghanistan is once again literally light years ahead of the best civilian trauma centres in the western world. As Nightingale took with her the experiences of war to better civilian care, modern military nurses are doing exactly the same today.

The lessons that she learned in the Crimean War, she brought to St Thomas' hospital, for example, in the design of the wards in the South Wing—the Nightingale wards. They may be old fashioned today but, at the time, they were world class. Their essence—the concept of light and air, good sight lines so that nurses can see their patients, the distance between the beds— so many of the things Nightingale introduced to nursing and care still hold true.

The Museum at St Thomas' Hospital is just one aspect of the strength of Florence Nightingale's lasting impact. Situated on the site of the first training school, it is at the heart of the way her legacy is communicated throughout the world.

A Professional Identity for the Twenty-first Century

Defining a nurse today is complicated by the variation in requirements for certification from one country to the next, and by the different levels of practice within nursing.

The designation of professional nurse is generally reserved for Registered Nurses (RNs), which the International Council of Nurses defines as people who have completed a nursing education programme and are qualified and authorised in their country to practice as a nurse.[20] In most countries, RNs complete between 16 and 19 years of education in total, including three to five years of nursing after their general secondary schooling. However, some countries require as few as 12 years total education. National professional nursing associations approve education programmes for RNs.[21]

There is a good deal of variation in terms of where this education is obtained. Until the 1970s, nurse education was provided mainly in hospitals. The current mixture of hospital, college and university programmes reflects attempts to upgrade and standardise requirements while keeping nursing education accessible. The balancing act is causing a great deal of debate in many parts of the world, especially as more countries adopt the university degree as the basis for nurse certification.

In a 2009 column he wrote for the *British Journal of Nursing*, Sir George Castledine, Professor and Consultant of Nursing at the Institute of Ageing and Health at Birmingham and Sussex Health Care, addressed concerns that university education would produce nurses who were 'too posh to wash', who could 'theorise but not catheterise'. "When I completed my nursing training I was trained to watch what went on around me, and to know all the answers based on ritual and routine. When I went to university they taught me to question all these answers, and to find out what I did not already know through research. As Kant famously wrote, 'Experience without theory is blind, but theory without experience mere intellectual play.'"[22]

Even as acceptance of the new norm increases, universities are struggling to increase capacity. US nursing schools turned away 49,948 qualified applicants from baccalaureate and graduate nursing programmes in 2008, mainly due to insufficient numbers of faculty. Other countries face similar problems.[23]

Along with RNs, most countries also have large and growing numbers of nurses who have less professional education than RNs but work alongside them within a more restricted scope of practice. They are variously called licensed practical nurses, enrolled nurses, healthcare assistants, assistant practitioners, nursing assistants or aides. Among non-professional nurses, some go through standardised educational programmes and are licensed, while others train at vocational schools and are not registered or licensed.

Nurse with an IV drip.

Nurse monitors a patient at her bedside.

Categories of Nurse

The nursing profession gradually stratified as educational and licensing requirements changed over the last 40 years. The definitions below are specific to the United States, but similar categories can be found in other countries. [24]

Registered Nurse (RN)
Scope of Practice

+ Teach patients and their families how to manage their illnesses or injuries.

+ Promote general health by educating the public.

+ Run screening or immunisation clinics and blood drives.

+ Establish a care plan or contribute to an existing plan.

+ Administer medication, check of dosages and avoid interactions.

+ Start, maintain, and discontinue intravenous (IV) lines.

+ Administer therapies and treatments.

+ Observe the patient and record those observations.

+ Consult with physicians and other healthcare clinicians.

+ Provide direction to licensed practical nurses and nursing aides.

Education

+ Bachelor's degree (four years at university).

+ Associate degree (two to three years in community or junior college).

+ Diploma from an approved nursing programme (three years in hospital, now very rare).

+ All nursing education programmes include classroom instruction and supervised clinical experience in hospitals.

Licensing

+ Graduates must then complete a national licensing examination in order to obtain a nursing license and qualify for entry-level positions as staff nurses.

Advancement Opportunities

+ Significant for university educated RNs.

+ More limited for associate degree and diploma holders. The US has made efforts to facilitate the upgrading from associate to bachelor's degrees.

Employment

+ 2.6 million working in the US in 2008.

+ 60 per cent of RN jobs are in hospitals, eight per cent in physician offices, five per cent in home care, five per cent in nursing care facilities.

+ 21 per cent of RNs are union members.

+ Median annual wages (2008): US $62,450.

+ Highest wages (2008): US $92,240.

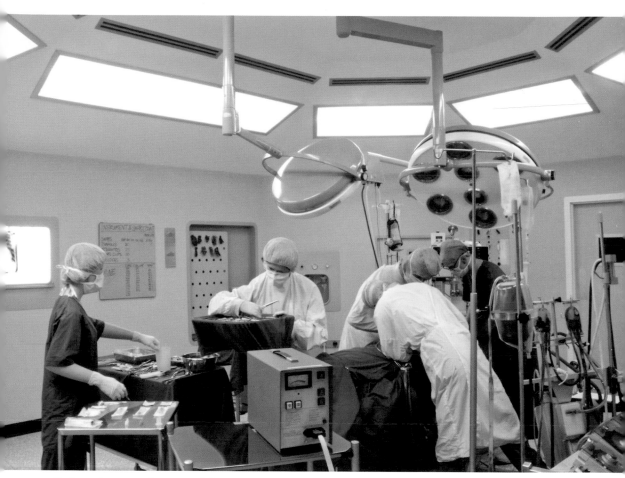

Doctors and nurses work as a team during surgery.

Advanced Practice Nurse (APN)
Scope of Practice

+ Everything RNs do.

+ Prescribe some medications.

+ Work autonomously.

Education

+ Master's degree in specialized program as clinical nurse specialists, nurse anesthetists, nurse-midwives, and nurse practitioners.

Employment

+ Work independently or in collaboration with physicians and can prescribe certain medications.

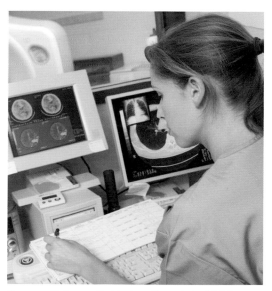

Nurse monitoring a patient having a Computerised Axial Tomography (CAT) scan.

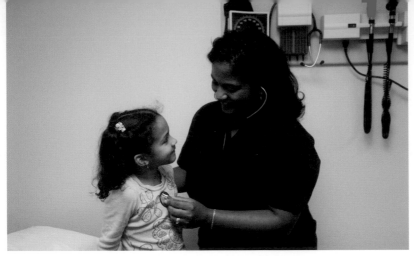

Nurse examines a child.

Licensed Practical Nurses (LPN)
Scope of Practice

+ Provide basic bedside care under direction of a physician or RN.

+ Measure and record patients' vital signs.

+ Prepare and give injections and enemas, monitor catheters, dress wounds, and give alcohol rubs and massages.

+ Assist with bathing, dressing, personal hygiene and moving around.

+ Feed patients who need help eating.

+ May supervise nursing aides.

+ Collect samples for testing.

+ Perform routine laboratory tests.

+ Record food and fluid intake and output.

+ Clean and monitor medical equipment.

+ Help physicians and registered nurses perform tests and procedures.

+ Monitor patients and report adverse reactions to medications or treatments.

+ Take health histories.

+ Complete insurance forms, pre-authorisations, and referrals.

+ Share information with RNs and doctors.

Education

+ One-year state-approved training program at vocational school, community or junior college.

+ High school diploma usually required for entry.

+ Combines classroom and clinical practice.

Licensing

+ Licensed by the National Council of State Boards of Nursing.

Opportunities for Advancement

+ In nursing homes, can advance to become charge nurses who oversee the work of other LPNs and nursing aides.

+ Can specialise in areas such as IV therapy, gerontology, long-term care, and pharmacology.

+ A number of educational institutions offer LPN-to-RN training programmes.

Employment

+ 753,600 LPN jobs in 2008.

+ 25 per cent in hospitals, 25 per cent in nursing care facilities, 12 per cent in physician offices and the rest in home healthcare and other settings.

+ Median annual wage (2008): US $39,030.

+ Highest wage (2008): US $53,580.

Nursing Assistants
Scope of Practice

+ Help patients to eat, dress, and bathe.

+ Answer calls for help.

+ Deliver messages.

+ Serve meals.

+ Make beds and tidy rooms.

+ Help patients get out of bed and walk.

+ Escort patients to operating and examining rooms.

+ Provide skin care.

+ Set up equipment, store and move supplies.

+ Assist with some procedures.

Education

+ High schools and vocational-technical centres.

+ Specific qualifications vary by occupation, State laws, and work setting.

Licensing

+ Nursing assistants working in nursing care facilities must meet federal government requirements, complete 75 hours of State-approved training and pass a competency evaluation. They are designated as certified nurse assistants (CNAs) and are placed on the State registry.

Opportunities for Advancement

+ Limited without additional education.

Employment

+ 1,470,000 nursing aides working in the US.

+ Very strong growth (up to 19 per cent) in employment anticipated over next ten years.

+ Median annual wage (2008): US $23,850.

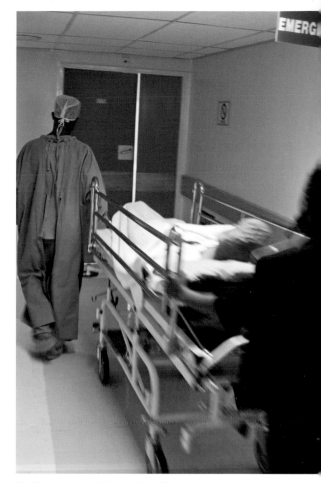

Healthcare personnel transport a patient.

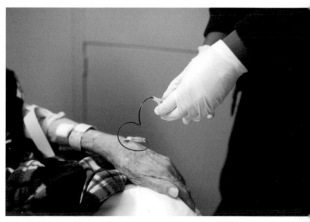

Nurse getting a blood sample from an elderly man.

Nurse Education
Moves Out of the Hospital

Dr Helen Mussallem was Director of Nursing Education at the Vancouver General Hospital when, in 1957, she was asked by the Canadian Nurses' Association to conduct a survey of nursing schools across Canada. Her report "Spotlight on Nursing Education" would transform nursing education. Now in her 90s and living down the road from the Canadian Nurses Association offices in Ottawa, where she served as Executive Director for almost 20 years, Dr Mussallem spoke to us about that critical moment in the professionalisation of nursing.

Until the late 1950s, nurses were educated in hospital-based nurse training programmes. Towards the end of the 50s, the National League for Nursing in the United States started working toward developing common accreditation standards for nurse education programmes. The Canadian Nurses Association (CNA) likewise started to give the issue of educational standards more thought.

The CNA asked Helen Mussallem, by that time a Master of Nursing with long experience as Director of Nursing Education at the Vancouver General Hospital, wartime sister and operating room nurse, to survey the hospital schools of nursing across Canada. Her mandate was to see whether they would meet the standards of a voluntary national accreditation programme. She visited 25 hospital training programmes across the country, conducting in-depth interviews and compiling information on all aspects of the programmes.

"I was truly appalled by what I saw in some of the hospitals," Mussallem remembers. "They were using student nurses as indentured labour." Held against the standards being established by the CNA for accreditation, only four of the 25 programmes would have measured up.

The CNA published her report, "Spotlight on Nursing Education"in 1960.[25] It had just four recommendations.
1. That a re-examination of the whole field of nursing education be undertaken.
2. That a school improvement programme be initiated to assist schools in upgrading their education programmes.
3. That a programme be established for evaluating the quality of nursing service in the areas where students in schools of nursing receive their clinical experience.
4. That a programme of accreditation for schools of nursing be developed by the CNA.

The report was greeted with vocal protests from, among others, the Canadian Hospital Association, as hospitals depended on the labour of student nurses to function. But it marked a point of no return.

Mussallem worked out the implementation strategy in her doctoral dissertation at Columbia University, which was published by the CNA in 1962. *Path to Quality: A Plan for the Development of Nursing Education Programs within the General Education System of Canada* became the blueprint for action as Mussallem was made Executive Director of the CNA and worked to dramatically change the training of Canadian nurses.

Mussallem considers that the US was likely ahead in early efforts to move nurse education out of the hospitals, but that the actual transition was much faster in Canada, despite the fact that changes needed to be made separately in each of Canada's ten provinces.

In an address to the King's Fund Seminar of Nurses in 1974, Mussallem surveyed the immense progress made in Canada since her report. "In 1966, only one of the 173 initial diploma programs was within the general educational system. That year, it admitted 21 students, less than one per cent of the total admissions to diploma programs in the country. In 1973, 8,248 students were admitted to diploma programs within the educational system, a figure that represents 77 per cent of the total number of students." Many of the programmes were offered within the Community College system.

By 1974, there were also 22 basic four to five-year programmes in university schools of nursing, leading to a Bachelor's degree in nursing.

As nursing students moved out of the hospitals, the need for nursing assistants grew sharply. These were not diploma nurses, but followed a ten to 18 month programme of training. By 1973, Mussallem cited, there were 60,000 nursing assistants practicing in Canada.

In Canada, at least, the era of hospital-based training programmes had come to an end.

Helen Mussallem as a nursing student at Vancouver General Hospital.

Dr Andrea Baumann (back right) with graduating nurses at The Aga Khan University in Pakistan, 2000.

A Global Look at Nursing Education

Dr Andrea Baumann, Director of the World Health Organization Collaborating Centre for Primary Health Care Nursing and Co-Director of the Nursing Health Services Research Unit at the McMaster University School of Nursing, assesses the global impact of recent changes in nursing education.

Throughout the years, the curriculum for nurses has expanded to include knowledge stemming from both technological and scientific advances. Nursing education has also evolved in response to increased globalisation. In most countries, the number of students in nursing education has grown as governments at all levels strive to advance healthcare. However, nursing curriculum and the status of nurses and their profession have varied—and continue to do so—depending on the prevailing national view.

Traditionally, nursing curriculum was delivered in hospitals and regarded as an apprenticeship. Early in their training, nurses were placed on hospital wards and provided the service component while they received basic education. Over time these basic courses varied from two to four years in length and resulted in a nursing diploma. In the early years, the curriculum was inductive and provided the basic principles of nursing, but the information evolved largely from the healthcare needs of the day. Nurses were taught essential technical and assessment skills, as well as nursing practices that ensured patient comfort and restoration of health.

During the past century, the need for complex care evolved. This was largely due to advances in basic science and greater understanding of both the mechanisms of disease processes and the importance of health promotion. It became evident in many countries that nurses required more advanced education. The curriculum had to provide additional information, include modern educational approaches, and address societal changes. Formal education for nurses began to take place outside the hospital setting in dedicated schools of nursing. These institutions varied around the world and included stand-alone nursing schools, public health schools, community colleges, and universities.

In countries like Canada and the US, movement towards diploma and degree education for nurses increased the demand for nurse educators. It also increased the need for these educators to have advanced degrees to help expand the scientific basis for the provision of nursing care. As nurse educators and nurse researchers developed, curricula began to include evidence-based healthcare and nursing theory and consider the inherent complexities of the nursing role, the synergy between nurses and other members of the healthcare profession, and the need for nurse leaders.

This broader focus reflects the evolution of nursing practice and is reflected in the efforts of various organisations to offer a more accurate and comprehensive definition of contemporary nursing. For example, the International Council of Nurses (ICN) states that "nursing encompasses autonomous and collaborative care".[26] The American Nurses' Association (ANA) emphasises that "nursing is the protection, promotion, and optimization of health and abilities", and the Royal College of Nursing (RCN) highlights "the use of clinical judgment in the provision of care".[27]

Unfortunately, changes in nursing curriculum and re-evaluation of nurses as key contributors to the healthcare system have not occurred worldwide. In many countries diploma education remains the standard, while in other countries nursing education has not moved past the aide level and nursing is still considered a lesser vocation.

Designation Difficulties

The designation of nurse is not a legal one. Nursing is a regulated profession in some countries and the title can be used only by practitioners who have successfully completed an approved curriculum and a national or state exam. In other countries, however, the term is used liberally. This causes a great deal of confusion, particularly in a global sense, as to what it means to be a nurse and what qualifications and education are necessary to fulfill this role.[28]

The globalisation of nursing has prompted an intense comparative look at nursing education and qualifications as nurses move beyond their geographical boundaries. During the past decade, nurse migration and mobility have increased in response to nursing shortages. Some countries, including the Philippines, have upgraded nursing education and curriculum so that nurses educated in-country can be employed in other countries where their services are in high demand. Many of these receiving countries have strict practice regulations and procedures.

Investments in Nursing

The development of nursing has been synonymous with the economic growth of countries and increased emphasis on health of the population. In countries that have strong health provisions, the medical and nursing workforce has expanded to meet national health needs and the nursing profession has gained in status.

Countries with a strong healthcare vision recognise that nurses provide an essential service. Thus the work environment, salary structure, and career path of nurses have improved. Initiatives to attract and retain nurses have made nursing an attractive career choice.

In countries where there has not been a significant investment in health services, the nursing profession has not grown at the same rate. Doctors outnumber nurses by an appreciable percentage in many countries and are often underemployed. Organisations such as the Pan American Health Organization (PAHO) and the World Health Organization (WHO) document the shortage of nurses and the lack of nursing educational institutions while noting the ever-increasing number of medical schools. Many countries have inadequate services for the size of their population.

However, there has been an impressive expansion of nursing education, both within and across countries.[29] Escalating labour market demands in developing countries have brought to light the importance of transnational education. The internet has increased access to education and made it possible for individuals to improve their qualifications and become competitive in the world market. However, this has also raised concerns about the quality of education being offered.

Many destination countries for foreign-trained nurses have made a considerable investment in educational initiatives to ensure the nurses are properly integrated into the healthcare system. At the present time, however, there is no international authority to monitor educational standards worldwide.[30] Related efforts by various international and national nursing bodies are being aided by cooperative ventures like the Bologna Process, which aims to make academic standards more comparable throughout Europe.[31] These types of evolving accords put pressure on source countries to change and enhance their educational systems.

Growing Interest in Nursing

The growing demand for nursing services in an ever-changing complex environment is an ongoing issue. There is tension in some countries between the need for a highly educated nursing workforce and efforts to decrease the cost of healthcare.[32] This has heightened international awareness of the value of nurses as human capital. In response, some countries have developed educational institutions to export nurses to other countries where their services are required. However, simply investing in human capital is not enough. Nursing education must be standardised to facilitate a common understanding of nursing practice and the role of nurses, which will help ensure the well-being of patients and the integrity of the healthcare system.

Nursing remains an attractive profession in countries where working conditions and wage structures have improved and continue to do so. In times of economic recession, occupations experiencing shortages are particularly appealing because of future employment possibilities. Market demand and improved work environments influence the numbers joining the profession. There is evidence that applications to nursing programmes are increasing in many countries. The application pool is changing with more men and people with second degrees applying to enter nursing programmes. But it has to be emphasised this is not occurring in all countries. There remains considerable work to be done to create consistent professional standards and enhance the nursing profession worldwide.

Reclaiming Independent Practice

Kelly Knoll, RN, NP, belongs to a bridge generation in Canadian nursing. It crosses the dramatic shift from high nursing unemployment in the 1990s to acute shortages the next decade, the transition from college to university entry to practice requirements, and finally the rapid introduction in her province of nurse practitioner roles. Through her story we see a profession defining itself for today's society.

"Nursing was not my first choice of career, to the extent that I was even thinking about a career when I finished high school with barely passing grades. But my grandmother used to tell us these fabulous stories about being a public health nurse for the school board. What drew me to nursing was the idea of being that kind of nurse, working independently outside of an institution."

Nursing Education in Transition

Kelly Knoll knew that public health nursing would require a university degree, and had some serious catching up to do. She was looking at a five-year programme: three years of community college to obtain her RN, then two years of university.

In the first year, she was introduced to bedside care, primarily in chronic care wards. Students would be assigned a patient and given two days to study the diagnosis and prepare.

"My first patient was a woman who had had a stroke", Knoll recalls. "She was on about 25 different medications and I spent the day crushing them up and feeding them to her. She smelled and could not communicate and was completely dependent. It was yuck. But after one full shift, I got to love that patient."

Half the class dropped out in the first year. "A lot of them found the experience too raw. And frightening to think we could all end up there, dependent on other people just to breathe."

Second year introduced students to more acute hospital work, and third year focused on mental health and bedside care again, only now they had not one patient, but ten. Of the 100 students who started the college programme with Knoll, only 40 graduated as RNs, and ten went on to complete a university degree.

Knoll's impulse after gradating college and obtaining her RN was to head into ICU nursing: "That was the cat's meow in nursing at the time: one patient per nurse. No one's pooing because they're barely alive. Everything's on monitors, the tubes are in. There's nothing you need to do on assessment skills alone. You're completely dependent on technology. I hated it."

Against all odds (and with the help of a relative) she obtained a summer replacement position in an NICU, received 16 days of orientation and worked a total of four shifts all summer. "There was no work. It was 1994, the peak of the nursing surplus. I was 22 years old, ready to work night and day, and begged the Director of Nursing for a job on the chronic care ward, even just to go on call and replace people when they were sick, but no."

That fall she started at Ottawa University and worked part-time at the Ottawa General Hospital. "If there's one thing I know how to do it is get a job, so I just harassed people until I found something. The competition was very tight and you had to really impress these nurse managers. I had done exceptionally well at college, top of my class. But the interviews were incredibly tough, touching on nursing philosophy and every possible eventuality: what would you do if a patient complained of chest pain, if air got into the IV line, if a chest tube came out.... There are no interviews like this anymore. It was because there were no jobs."

She was hired to be on call throughout the hospital. She would start on one floor and then an hour into her shift move to another floor with ten new patients, and on it went. "Today, when you graduate", says Knoll, "you're mentored for an entire year, but I was on my own and the number of mistakes I made is so terrifying that I still have dreams I've forgotten someone in the hall." The environment was chaotic and impossibly demanding. "You were monitoring one patient post-heart attack, another was on a ventilator—I'd never looked after a patient on a ventilator as a student—the next on peritoneal dialysis and the next had had a bilateral amputation, suffered from dementia and was climbing out of bed. Restraints were not used as they were

Kelly Knoll, NP, going to work at the Sherwood Observation and Detention Centre where she provides health services to young offenders.

considered "bad" at the time. So that guy falls, and the next one's catheter falls out. The person with chest pain was actually having another heart attack. One nurse for ten patients in a cutthroat environment with no one to help you."

There was much disdain for university nurses among the hospital nurses, who knew they had until the year 2000 to obtain their degree, called a "post-RN", to have any possibility of promotion in the future. "Nurses who had gone through institution-based training programs despised this new generation that was forcing them to go back to school", Knoll recalls, "and I represented that. These nurses had never been to college or university. They could run an entire floor, but were hopelessly intimidated by university classes and literature searches."

Working hard, taking shifts and helping friends are what make your reputation as a nurse.

Knoll persisted with the university programme, but nursing had lost its appeal. The one redeeming experience was a four-month tour in community health centres in her very last term. But when she graduated there were no jobs. Many of her classmates from college were working low-end, labour intensive jobs in nursing homes or replacement shifts in hospitals. Knoll married and moved a number of times over the next few years. In every city the story was the same: if there was a job to be had, the entire city was lined up to get it. She trained as a massage therapist and did that for a while.

Back in Ottawa in 1996 with a young son, Knoll went to work part-time in the NICU, but her earlier discomfort with the very particular skills resurfaced and she left to have her second baby with no intention of returning.

A Taste of Independence

The area of nursing that attracted her back was palliative care, which despite the anguish and sheer physical demands, Knoll enjoyed and felt very confident in. She started on the hospital palliative care unit and appreciated the independence and the feeling of being in control. Her massage skills were put to good use. "I learned a tremendous amount about pain control, got to know the patients and their families at a very meaningful time, and appreciated how much we could do as nurses without a doctor involved."

From there, she moved to a hospice in her neigbourhood, where nurses worked even more independently. "It was generally just us and the families caring for people in their final days." She liked teaching families how to touch and interact, and how to perform various aspects of her job.

"Pain and symptom management was all done without monitors at the hospice", says Knoll. "That is why I started to respect the bed bath again. I could see how close a patient was to death when I washed them by the colour of their skin and the way they felt."

Knoll then became coordinator of the hospice, away from direct care. She struggled initially because her bedside care abilities were a point of pride. But there was a new challenge in matching up people's needs with the services available in the hospitals, hospices and other places. She would visit patients in hospital and determine whether the hospice was appropriate for them.

Knoll then worked as a clinical care coordinator for palliative and complex continuing care, deciding which patients should be in each type of facility within the city of Ottawa Local Health Integration Network (LHIN). The new structure took decision-making power away from local institutions such as the hospice and put in in the hands of the LHIN, and Knoll became central dispatch. Part of the job was assessing how close a person was to death, and she would do rounds at various centres. "That was the most political job I've ever held. Because it is all about funding: if someone takes three days longer than expected to die in a hospital bed, that is just more money. I was good at it and it was a great job for a nurse, determining yes or no based on clinical findings. But I did no family care, no patient care and it was very stressful." And it did not make her very popular among many of her former colleagues.

"The day I got accepted into the nurse practitioner program, I resigned."

Becoming a Nurse Practitioner

Knoll had learned about the nurse practitioner role back in college as it was making a bit of a comeback in the 1990s in Canada and was commonplace in the US. When she was still single, she thought she might someday move to the US and work as a nurse practitioner. Her experience with the independence of palliative care work had reinforced the drive.

The University of Ottawa had a two-year full time Nurse Practitioner programme. Knoll feels privileged that her husband's income allowed her to take the time away from work. Most of the nurses in the programme were older, had some money and a leave of absence from their job. Only two, including Knoll, still had young kids. "One woman was a full time ICU nurse, and a farmer, and had six kids. With her experience in the ICU and with medication, she aced every exam, but she was intimidated by computers and literature searches, so we helped her on her papers."

Training involved three days of fieldwork and two days of classroom every week. In the first year Knoll developed a chronic disease management programme, in a Family Health Team. "I had to put together the whole program, from the needs assessment to getting the funding. You pass or fail according to whether you can put a program together. They were teaching us to step up. Do not wait for people to build clinics. Look around at what's needed in the community and get it done with your community partners. If you cannot find a job, make a job. I felt like I was Einstein after that. I was so proud to be able to get my own funding."

Knoll found the programme completely different from anything she had done before. "It was medicine. The pathophysiology was vaguely familiar, but the diagnosis, assessment and therapeutics were all brand new." When called on to put these to use, she found she could fall back on her nursing skills while she got comfortable in the newer parts of the role. "Confronted with a woman in the ER with vaginal bleeding from a miscarriage, I could start with counseling about losing a baby (a familiar nursing role) while formulating the clinical (ie doctor) questions I had to run through. As a nurse, you're not used to asking those in systematic order. But you can start with the 'touch' to get them comfortable."

She worked with homeless people at a mission, in primary care at a Family Health Team, at a downtown immigrant health clinic, in well-woman well-baby care, and spent three months doing physicals in a hypertension clinic. "You learn to go head to toe and ask all the necessary screening questions. You're learning from the doctor and perform like a med student. Doctors generally are fabulous teachers—it is part of their profession—and those who accept NP trainees are better than most. Hospital doctors appear much more appreciative of the acute care NPs but doctors in the community see more overlap and we have not quite figured out how to define that. We're competing for income in the community, at least until the doctors go on salary as well."

She was one of 22 graduates in 2009, a year when some 200 NPs graduated across Ontario. "The past five years have seen a major resurgence in interest in NPs and I'm right in the middle of it. The jobs have opened up with positions in Family Health Teams and NP-run clinics. It has been accepted."

Knoll learned how to create her own job. After graduating, she volunteered at the Newgate Residential Addiction Treatment Centre that previously had one visiting doctor who would perform very quick physicals on new arrivals. Knoll wanted to provide more extensive assessments and the centre agreed to take her on as a volunteer one day a week for three

months on a trial basis. After four weeks
they hired her.

She also now works at the Youth Service
Bureau of Ottawa, in a position that keeps
expanding as she can demonstrate needs,
propose ways to meet them and demonstrate
benefit. It involves going beyond the simple
intake assessment to providing ongoing care for
a very difficult group of youth incarcerated for
serious crimes. Knoll also recognises the value
of documenting the services provided and their
results, which helps to improve services but also
recognises the NP role. Knoll has since been
hired at another larger youth facility and, most
recently at a crisis unit that intervenes when
children at risk are being removed from their
homes. "This is the crucial moment, when the
family crisis has just peaked", says Knoll, "and
there are tremendous opportunities to help as
an NP."

Word about what a nurse practitioner does
is getting around thanks to this new crop of
graduates who have taken on a leadership role
and are opening up new ground for nursing.
Knoll repeats words she has said a thousand
times before and will say a thousand times more.

**A nurse practitioner is a
registered nurse who has
additional knowledge and
training to perform assessment
and diagnostic procedures and
treat, diagnose and prescribe
for more common episodic
illnesses and more complex
mental health illnesses across
the spectrum.**

Propriety in Nursing

Zena Edmund-Charles, RN, MBE trained as a midwife in Kingston, Jamaica before coming to England in 1956 to pursue her career. In 1996 she was awarded the MBE for services to community nursing. She talked to us about nurse training in an earlier time when perfection in dress, manner and the caring environment were an integral part of nurse identity.

"I enjoyed my working days in hospital. Many of the student nurses and even some staff nurses could not cope with the strict discipline on and off the wards and, for this reason, would give up their training or travel back to their homeland. I had no problem with discipline, and came into this with one thing in mind, come what may, and that was to pursue a career in nursing. My parents were very strict, so my upbringing was a strict one. Discipline, honesty, time and respect were never allowed to be forgotten, not even for one minute.

Through the years I had several favourite patients. Some of these patients would refuse to be treated by other nurses because they were heavy handed, but I put myself in their position and treated them as I would want to be treated.

All ranks of nursing staff had to be properly dressed at all times when on duty. Well-pressed striped blue and white dresses, shining white and well-starched aprons and caps, black stockings, black lace up shoes with rubber heels. Hair had to be up off the shoulders and collars, nails clipped short and clean, no jewellery, no wrist watches, starched belts—colour according to the year the student was in. Each grade had its own colour belt. Matron wore green and the sisters were all in blue dresses with long sleeves, and would wear white frilled, elastic cuffs when they rolled their sleeves up to perform a duty in nursing. If the cap was not folded in a way that it looked like the bakers' hat, you would be asked to remove it from your head and then the sister would re-fold it. Nurses also had to report on and off duty to the dining room at meal times on the dot of time. Late? Never.

If you should report being sick, the Nurses' Home Sister would check your temperature and, if there was no temperature, off to the ward you go. You would not be considered to be ill. Some of the girls knew how to beat the sister. When she was due to visit them, these girls would put hot water, tea or food in their mouth, hence the reading of the thermometer would show a high temperature. They were never found out.

All nurses had to be in by 9.30pm. The porter would lock the gates at this time. If a nurse wanted to come in later than 9.30pm, she would have to ask the matron for a late night pass which allowed her to come in through the gates no later than 10.30pm. The Irish girls had to go dancing every night at the Lyceum and 10.30pm was too early for bed, so they got friendly with the gate porter who would let them in whenever, until the night sister caught up with them coming in later than permitted. They were reprimanded by the matron and no more late passes given. So what did these girls do? They managed to cut a hole large enough in the wire fence behind the nurses home and from thence they had a whale of a time going in and out as they pleased.

Everyone had to have a handle on their can (an old West Indian saying). All had to be addressed correctly: Mr, Mrs, Miss, Ms, Sister, Staff Nurse or nurse. Very rarely the night sister would be heard calling a very ill patient by his or her Christian name. The consultants are Mr or Mrs; Junior nurses did not have much to do with the Registrar or consultants. The clerical, domestic and porters all had to be addressed properly... that is good old fashioned respect.

Nursing and caring for the patient and their families was a serious business. No messing around or cheap talk and laughter around those being cared for were permitted. That did not say we could not have a quick chatter and laugh with patients providing no one was awaiting any attention. We were little devils when the cat was away and there was much good clean fun with the patients who were up to it. They were devilish themselves and on sister's return they, like us, were perfect angels; butter would not melt in their mouths.

No one was allowed to sit on the beds, not even the patients could sit or lie on top; they had to sit on the chair or be in bed properly. No dirty utensils could be seen hanging about

Zena Edmund-Charles with a young patient.

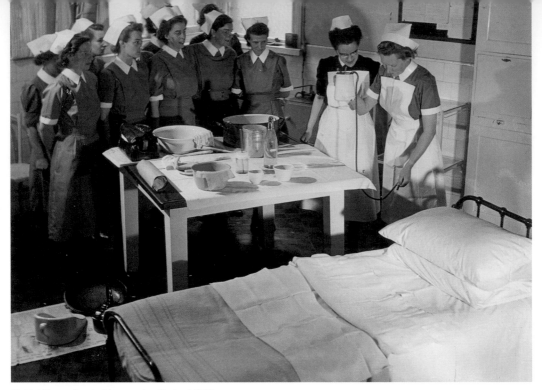
District Nurses in a training session, England, 1956.

on the bed, lockers or tables. Tablets, or any form of medication, were not allowed to be left on the bedside table if the patient was asleep or out of the ward (eg at X-Ray or physiotherapy). Pillows all had to be neat and tidy, with the mouth of the pillow cases turned away from the door, especially before the visitors came, or ward rounds.

The student nurses did much of the cleaning and dusting. Polishing the floor was done by using a heavy bumper, using a swinging movement. It was heavy—no hoover! The ward sister and Matron would run their fingers along the window sills and ledges in search of dust and dirt. If any was found, there would be hell to pay!

Although the coal fires were always burning there was never any dust or dirt to be seen. The nurses even had to clean the windows in the sterilising room. On weekends and Bank Holidays the student nurses spent much time cleaning the wheels of the bed. All fluff had to be removed using tweezers. The bed tables and lockers had to be scrubbed in and out.

At visiting times the patients who did not have visitors had to be made to feel wanted. The student nurses would sit with the patient and talk to them until all the visitors went. In those days, we did not have volunteers on whom we could depend to wash, feed or visit patients. The nurses had that in their daily duties. That is what we called nursing.

Our concern was not only for the patients but also for their loved ones, their families. Our patients were also number one in our lives, whether they were racist, uncouth or not. They had to be treated with respect and their dignity would not be taken from them. There were no mixed wards. Ladies were in their wards and men in theirs.

I thank God I did my training in those days, because all to do with nursing was perfect, and everyone concerned was interested in 100 per cent proper care and attention for whoever was in need of help. There was love and dedication from all, or most of us, who entered the field of caring, be it medical or nursing. I am proud to be a part of those days."[33]

A nurse in a starched cap and uniform, washing her hands in an improved, bacteria-controlled environment. The improvements include the tiled walls and the towel machine above the sink, USA, 1930s.

An advert for nursing outfits from *The American Journal of Nursing.*

The Uniform

The uniform has played an important role in nursing identity. The first real uniform in the UK was designed by a student of Florence Nightingale, who required primarily that the nurse's attire be simple, and dispense with any features of women's dress that could compromise quiet and cleanliness.

Uniforms evolved differently around the globe, but for much of the last century sought to convey visual information about a nurse's rank, training and hospital affiliation. The cap, apron, pin and piping were all important identifying features.

As nursing education moved out of the hospitals, there were attempts to standardise uniforms and they lost some of their particularities. Scrubs, previously worn only by surgical nurses, first became popular in the US in the 1990s and have since been adopted in other countries. Some hospitals have done away with uniforms almost completely.

The fidget of silk and of crinoline, the rattling of keys, the creaking of stays and of shoes, will do a patient more harm than all the medicines in the world will do him good.

Florence Nightingale, *Notes on Nursing*, 1860.

District Nurse helps a patient at home, England, 1962.

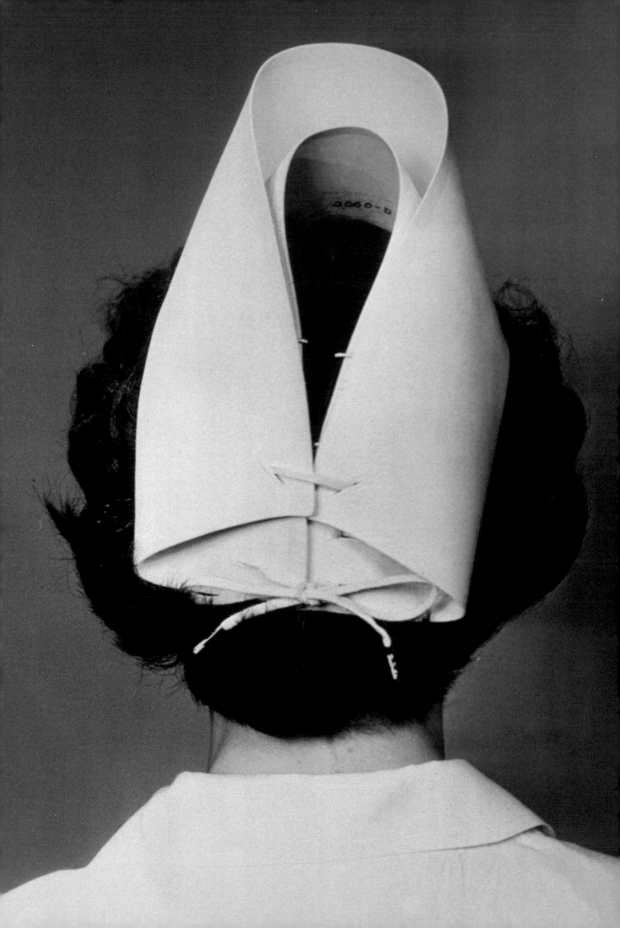

Anne Conrod, RN, Royal Victoria Hospital School of Nursing, Montréal, Canada, graduating in 1959.

1 Cap. Nurses in training earned the cap after completing their first year. It was awarded at a capping ceremony that marked the end of a nurse's probationary status. Schools of nursing use different designs of cap to distinguish their students from those of other hospitals. In 1959, the Royal Victoria Hospital cap was small, and plain white.

2 Pin. Nurses received their pin upon graduation. It bore the crest of the Royal Victoria Hospital.

3 Chest. The starched bib could be worn after the second year of training. At the Royal Victoria Hospital, graduate nurses were provided with an all white uniform that distinguished them from probationary nurses, who wore striped shirts.

OPPOSITE Nurse in starched cap, viewed from behind.

Graduating nurses in the Nurses' Residence at the Royal Victoria Hospital, Montréal, Canada, 1959.

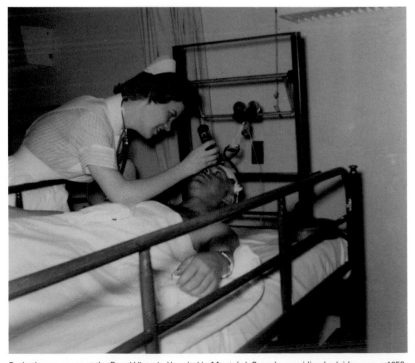

Probationary nurse at the Royal Victoria Hospital in Montréal, Canada, providing bedside care, c 1958. "Probies" were identified by their pink and white striped shirts.

Gondama Referral Center, outside of Bo, Sierra Leone: Swedish nurse Sara Eklöf checks a small patient at the Intensive Care Unit. In relief nursing, the logo on the t-shirt identifies the organisation a nurse is working for.

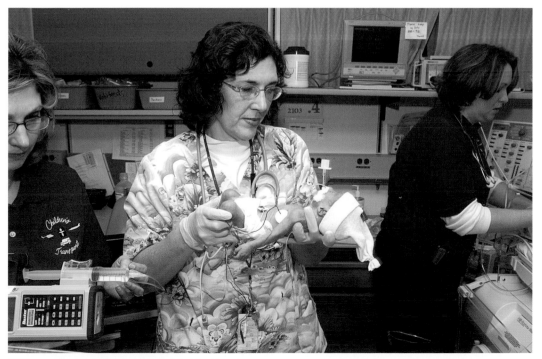

NICU nurse Susan Craig holds sextuplet Kyle Allen Hanselman.

2
Passport to the World

Passport to the World

Nursing is needed in all corners of the world and nurses have, throughout history, proven to be willing travelers and migrants. Many nurses are in fact attracted to the profession for the mobility it affords. In recent years, nurse migration has attracted much attention as the supply of nurses in source countries is depleted to levels that compromise the health of populations. And some measures have been taken to encourage responsible recruiting practices in the most popular destination countries. But nurses have always travelled, and will continue to move around the globe, sometimes visiting, other times settling in new countries. The ideal vision is an exchange of cultures, expertise and opportunity that enriches nursing and societies everywhere.

We have approached the issue of migration in this chapter from both global and personal perspectives. Mireille Kingma, a consultant with the International Council of Nurses, examines recent trends and the issues they raise for both source and destination countries. At a personal level, opportunities to work and sometimes settle abroad can be very appealing and the Commonwealth long provided a framework for migration that enabled nurses to train and work abroad with relative ease. We spoke with two nurses born in Trinidad and Jamaica who took a familiar route to the UK in the 1950s and 60s, as well as an Australian nurse who recently returned home after years of work in London. Former President of the International Council of Nurses, Christine Hancock, concludes the chapter with a look at the commonality among nurses and the challenges they face worldwide.

PREVIOUS PAGES Marites Cabreza, a nurse with the 354th Civil Affairs Brigade, tends to a patient during a medical civil action project in Djibouti, 2008.

A group of nurses from Base Hospital 21 on the deck of the SS Paul, May 1917.

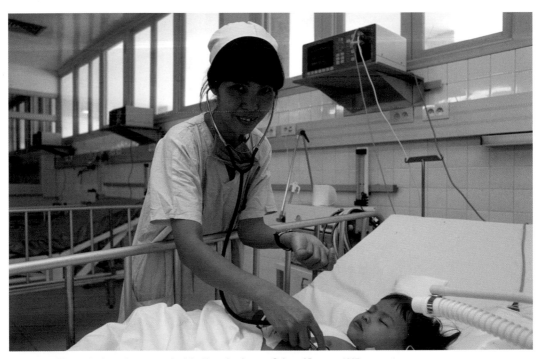

A nurse working at the intensive care unit of the Heart Institute at Saigon, Vietnam, 1997.

Nurses on the Move

Mireille Kingma, PhD, RN is a consultant for nursing and health policy with the International Council of Nurses, a federation of over 130 national nurses' associations. During the past 20 years she has been responsible for international consultations and training programmes in more than 60 countries. Her recent book, *Nurses on the Move: Migration and the Global Health Care Economy*, was released in 2006. The following text is adapted from an article she wrote for the *Online Journal of Issues in Nursing* in May, 2008.

The number of international migrants on the move each year continues to increase. While they represent a steady three per cent of the world's population, their numbers have doubled in the last four decades, now reaching a total of 191 million international migrants.[1] There has been a particularly marked growth in labour migration flows to industrialised countries and an increasing feminisation of migration flows, with women representing almost half of today's international migrants.[2] And many more women are now migrating independently of partners or families, thus changing family dynamics and community networks in both source and destination countries.[3] Women migrants are becoming agents of economic change as they enter the international labour market and participate in a new distribution of global wealth.[4]

Nurse migration occurs in this context of increasing global mobility and a growing competition for scarce skills, including skills needed in the healthcare sector. Migration in the context of a supply surplus can be considered a positive strategy to reduce unemployment, and improve the national economy through the transfer of funds between migrant workers and their families left behind (estimated to be US$ 232 billion in 2005).[5] However, in the healthcare sector, which faces critical staff shortages, international migration becomes a challenge that needs to be urgently addressed.

The international recruitment efforts to draw health professionals away from countries where the basic health needs of the population are not met affects the national workforce supply in these countries, an issue that increasingly appears on the political agenda.[6]

This text looks at the characteristics and the effects of nurse migration, explores the factors driving international nurse mobility, and discusses current issues in nurse migration. Given the critical shortage of health professionals willing to remain in active practice worldwide, it is argued that serious attention be given to retention strategies rather than restricting national and international recruitment.

The Numbers

The percentage of foreign-educated nurses working in Australia, Canada, the United Kingdom (UK) and the United States (US) is currently reported to be between five to ten per cent of these countries' nurse workforce. Thousands of nurses, the vast majority of them women, migrate each year in search of better pay and working conditions, career mobility, professional development, a better quality of life, personal safety, or sometimes just novelty and adventure.[7]

New Zealand reports that 21 per cent of its nurses are educated abroad, a significant increase in the last decade.[8] In Switzerland, 30 per cent of employed registered nurses are foreign-educated.[9] In 2005, 84 per cent of the new entrants to the Irish nursing register were

Greek trainee nurses in London, 1940s.

foreign-educated.[10] There is no doubt that foreign-educated nurses make a significant contribution to the delivery of healthcare in most industrialised countries and in many developing countries, with regional or sub-regional hubs, for example South Africa, attracting nurses from neighbouring countries by offering better pay, working conditions, and/or professional development opportunities.

Migration Patterns

Nurses are beginning to duplicate the 'carousel' pattern of migration long seen among physicians. They leave their source countries and migrate to several countries over the course of their professional lives, each time developing their skills and credentials until they reach the US, repeatedly identified as the epicentre of international migration.[11] For example, 40 per cent of the surveyed Filipino nurses employed in the UK had previously worked in Southeast Asia and the Middle East.[12] 43 per cent of working international nurses surveyed in London were considering relocating to another country, in many cases to the US.[13]

Historically, there has been a tendency for international nurse migration to be a North–North phenomenon (in which the place of origin and destination are both in industrialised countries) or a South–South phenomenon (in which the place of origin and destination are both in developing countries). However, it is estimated that 30,000 nurses and midwives educated in sub-Saharan Africa are now employed in seven OECD countries, specifically, Canada, Denmark, Finland, Ireland, Portugal, UK, and US.[14] This rapid growth in international recruitment from developing countries to industrialised countries has gained considerable media and policy attention in recent years.[15]

In 2000, more than twice the number of new graduates from nursing programmes in Ghana left that country for employment in industrialised countries.[16] In Malawi, between 1999 and 2001 over 60 per cent of the registered nurses in a single tertiary hospital (114 nurses) left for employment in other countries.[17] In 2003, a hospital in Swaziland reported that 30 per cent of their 125 nurses left to work abroad and, between 1999 and 2001, Zimbabwe lost 32 per cent of their registered nurses to employment in the UK.[18]

Migration patterns may be seen to change over time. More and more developing countries are contributing to the pool of international nurse migrants. The number of countries sending international nurse recruits to the UK increased from 71 in 1990 to 95 in 2001.[19] The Philippines, once the leading source of nurse migrants to Ireland and the UK, was outranked by India in 2005.[20] While Ireland was a nurse exporting country for decades, it is now an importing country recruiting mainly from the Philippines, Australia, India, South Africa and the US.[21]

Professionally active nurses are important players in an increasingly competitive and global labour market. Unable to meet domestic need and demand, many industrialised countries are looking abroad for a solution to their workforce shortages; the magnitude of current international recruitment is unprecedented.[22]

Unpacking the Nursing Shortage

It is important to look at nurse mobility within the context of the nursing shortage and to consider the paradox of unemployed nurses seen in the very countries with the greatest shortage, so as to understand how various societal forces contribute to nurse migration.

Nurses migrating from developing to industrialised countries often leave behind an already disadvantaged system. The nurses who remain assume heavier workloads and experience reduced work satisfaction and low morale contributing to high levels of absenteeism and a deteriorated quality of care delivery.[23] This in turn continues to feed the desire of health professionals to seek better working conditions, often outside their national boundaries.[24]

Nurse vacancy rates in industrialised countries are high.[25] In the US, 1.2 million new and replacement nurses will be needed by 2014.[26] Yet, within a context of shortage there are nurses, in both industrialised and developing countries, who are professionally qualified but without employment. This is a modern paradox, ie, nurses who are willing to work but who are refused posts by national health systems unable to absorb them, not for lack of need, but for lack of funds and/or health sector reform restrictions (eg payroll cuts or freezes imposed by international financial institutions or national government policy). In Kenya, although half of all nursing positions are unfilled, a third of all nurses are unemployed.[27] Recent nurse graduates from Uganda, Grenada, and Zambia are faced with unemployment, as their health systems do not have the funds to cover their salaries. Nurses in Tanzania, the Philippines, and parts of Eastern Europe are working for free in order to maintain their competencies and be next in line when a budgeted position becomes available.

Push and Pull Factors in Deciding to Migrate

There has been a great deal of discussion of the 'push' and 'pull' factors behind decisions to migrate.[28] Research continues to find the major reasons behind health worker migration are the pull factors of better remuneration, safer environment, improved living conditions in the destination countries, and the push factors of a lack of support from supervisors, non-involvement in decision making, lack of facilities, lack of promotions, lack of a future, and heavy workloads in their home countries.[29]

While financial incentive is not the only factor contributing to nurse migration, there is no doubt that it plays a key role in deciding whether or not to migrate. According to the International Organization for Migration (IOM), remaining in one's country of birth is the norm and many field studies confirm that most migrants would prefer to stay home in familiar surroundings and within their extended family.[30] Recent research suggests that the relative income of nurses within their home countries is a critical influence on attrition and migration rates.[31]

The substantial wage disparities found between nurses and other professional workers within the country are felt to be denigrating, a major source of frustration, and now a recognised motivating factor in attrition and international migration.[32]

Non-financial factors, such as political forces, poverty, age of the migrant, past colonial and cultural ties between source and destination countries, facilitated emigration process, employment/educational opportunities for family members, and existing diaspora (transnational communities), also play a very important role.[33] In one way or another, a better life and livelihood are at the root of decisions to migrate.[34]

Managing Migration

For nurses to practice their profession internationally, they need to meet both professional standards and migration criteria. In the interest of public safety, nurses' qualifications must be screened in a systematic way to ensure they meet the minimum professional standards of the country where they are to deliver care. Language is a crucial vehicle for the vital communication needed both between the patient and care provider, and also between members of the health team. It is not surprising that in many countries, a nurse's right to practice is limited if the foreign-educated nurse's language skills do not support safe care practices. History has

Students at the William Rathbone Staff College, Liverpool, England, 1960s.

demonstrated a tendency for migrant flows to be the strongest between source and destination countries that share a common language.[35]

Foreign nurses also need to meet national security and immigration criteria in order to enter the country and to stay on a permanent or temporary basis. There is no doubt that nurse mobility will be affected by national security concerns. For example a tightening of border restrictions after terrorism attacks or the opening of borders with new economic agreements, such as the expansion of the European Union, will continue to influence nurse migration patterns.

Negotiations to facilitate the temporary employment of foreign healthcare workers through the introduction of the General Agreement on Trade in Services (GATS) have not progressed. The future impact of this agreement on global nurse mobility is therefore unclear.[36] On the other hand, mutual recognition agreements that allow for automatic re-accreditation and that are often linked to an economic cooperation have encouraged nurse migration at the regional level. Examples of such agreements include Protocol II of the Caribbean Community and Common Market (CARICOM), the North American Free Trade Agreement (NAFTA), the Trans-Tasman Agreement, and Nursing Directives of the European Union.

Looking Ahead

There have been various attempts to reduce migration through legislation, national guidelines, or international agreements. Increasingly, however, it has been acknowledged that migration is a characteristic of today's globalised world and that such control mechanisms may have the perverse effect of infringing individuals' freedom of movement and exposing the recruitment process to even greater corruption and double standards. A delicate balance must be maintained between the human and labour rights of the individual and a collective concern for the health of a nation's population.

One of the most serious problems migrant nurses encounter in their new community and workplace is that of racism and its resulting discrimination.[37] Incidents are, however, often hidden by a blanket of silence and therefore difficult to quantify.[38] Migrant nurses are frequent victims of poorly enforced equal opportunity policies and pervasive double standards. If we recognise that international migration will continue and probably increase in coming years, the protection of workers is a priority issue and should be safeguarded in all policies and practices that affect migrant health professionals. Various codes of practice addressing ethical, international recruitment, or similar instruments, have been introduced at national and international levels. Their effectiveness, however, is yet to be demonstrated.[39]

Brain drain, which implies a loss to the source country of vital skills, professional knowledge, and management capacity, is only relevant as a concept if linked with permanent migration. In fact, there has been an increasing mix of temporary/permanent migration with a noted growth in temporary migration.[40] If migrants return to their home country (or the country that has invested in their education), they will once again be a national resource, and even an enriched resource if their acquired skills and knowledge are put to good use. Until we have better data, it is impossible to know if brain circulation, rather than brain drain, is the current reality. Brain circulation, however, definitely has the potential for being a 'best case' scenario for the future.

Migration is increasingly seen as a means for development and a better distribution of global wealth.[41] While some developing countries are "hemorrhaging" from nurse migration, others are benefiting from exchange programmes, by the channeling of remittances from nurses working abroad to public sector development projects in their source country, or finding migration a solution to high unemployment levels.[42] Industrialised countries faced with dramatic nurse shortages continue to see the recruitment of foreign-educated nurses as part of the solution to their failing health systems.

International mobility is a reality in a globalised world, one that will not be regulated out of existence. International migration is a symptom of the larger, systemic problems that make nurses leave their jobs and, at times, of the problems in a country's health sector. The data clearly show that no matter how attractive the pull factors of the destination country, little migration takes place without substantial push factors driving people away from the source country.[43] It can be difficult to determine which comes first—the recruitment factor or the wish to migrate.

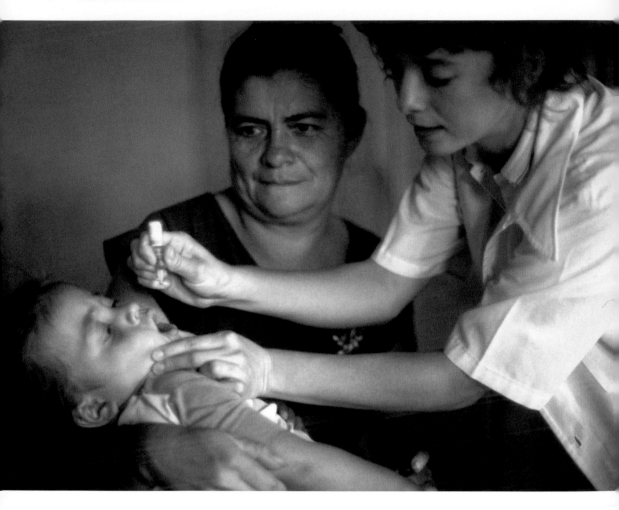

What Nurses Say About Migration

Paul Troy from Beaumont Hospital in Dublin, interviewed nurses and directors of nursing in Ireland and in source countries of foreign recruits working in Ireland.[44] His research was published in *Human Resources for Health* in 2007. Below are some of the things nurses had to say:

+ A nurses' right to migrate must be upheld, despite potential negative effects on the home country's health system.

+ Many source countries face lower quality care as a result of shortages.

+ Many nurses plan to go home.

+ None of the nurses planned to work in nursing when they returned home, partly because of the poor conditions in hospitals.

+ Foreign trained nurses assume less responsibility and display less autonomy than their Irish-trained counterparts, limiting upward mobility.

Pros and Cons of Nurse Migration

The International Council of Nurses summarises points commonly raised about the experience of international migration.[45]

Pros

+ Educational opportunities.

+ Professional practice opportunities.

+ Personal and occupational safety.

+ Better working conditions.

+ Improved quality of life.

+ Trans-cultural nursing workforce (eg racial and ethnic diversity).

+ Cultural sensitivity/competence in care.

+ Stimulation of nurse-friendly recruitment and contract conditions.

+ Personal development.

+ Global economic development.

+ Improved knowledge base and brain 'gain'.

+ Sustained maintenance and development of family members in the country of origin.

Cons

- Brain and/or skills drain.

- Closure of health facilities due to nursing shortages in a given area.

- Overwork of nurses practising in depleted areas.

- Potentially abusive recruitment and employment practices.

- Vulnerable status of migrants.

- Loss of national economic investment in human resource development.

Nurses for Export

The Philippines

Nurse migration is nothing new in the Philippines. Government support to train nurses for work overseas started in the 1950s. They were educated in English using a curriculum based on American nurse training. Filipino nurses are now the largest group of foreign-trained nurses in most destination countries. The country is unique in producing large numbers of surplus nurses at a level of education that meets the requirements of developed countries. By the year 2000, more than 250,000 Filipino-trained nurses were scattered across the globe, with the main destination countries including the UK, Saudi Arabia, Ireland, Singapore and the US. Fully 85 per cent of employed Filipino nurses were working outside their home country. And the outflow has picked up speed since then. A study of the recent evolution of nurse training in the Philippines found that the number of nursing schools in the country increased from 170 in 1999 to 470 in 2005. Over 70 per cent of nurse graduates leave the country to work abroad each year.[46]

The main impetus behind the programme is the remittances that workers abroad send back to their families. In 2004, the Central Bank of the Philippines reported total remittances of US$8.5 billion from all workers abroad, representing 10 per cent of the country's gross domestic product (GDP). The International Council on Nurse Migration found these amounts to be rising rapidly: to $10 billion in 2005, $12.8 in 2006 and $14.7 billion in 2007.[47] Nurses are more likely than other workers to send money home (95 per cent reported doing so in one study) and most send more than 25 per cent of their income back, usually to parents and siblings.[48]

Government does far more than train nurses for overseas work. The Philippine Overseas Employment Administration works to promote Filippino workers to foreign countries, regulate recruitment agencies, reduce the cost of emigrating and the hassle of completing travel papers. It also monitors the treatment of Filipino workers overseas. Another government organisation, the Overseas Workers' Welfare Administration prepares people for departure, provides advice on the best ways to send money home and protects workers overseas, with legal services and resource centres abroad. Its work is funded in part by a small membership fee paid by all departing workers.[49]

More recently, the Philippines government has taken steps to attract workers back. According to the 2006 World Health Organization (WHO) report, returnees are offered tax-free shopping for a year, loans for business capital and subsidised scholarships.[50]

Some international observers are concerned that the ever-increasing demand for Filippino nurses is depleting the health system in the Philippines of nurses and lowering the quality of care as the number of nursing positions that remain unfilled in the Philippines grows.[51]

India and China, as well as Russia appear to be following the example and are ramping up training of nurses to work abroad. Looking at the Filippino experience, the World Bank recommends these countries take similar measures to manage international migration. These measures include:

+ Regulate private recruitment agencies to ensure the validity of contracts.

+ Prepare citizens prior to departure.

+ Protect migrant workers abroad.

+ Develop a recording mechanism to identify emigrants.

+ Promote competition in the remittances industry to lower transaction costs and increase benefits for home families.[52]

Why Do Indian Nurses Emigrate?
(And What Would It Take to Keep Them at Home?)

In an article published in the *International Nursing Review* in 2006, Nursing Sister Philomina Thomas from the All India Institute of Medical Sciences, New Delhi, looked at some of the factors behind the increase in nurse migration from India.[53] She found that dissatisfaction with working conditions and with social attitudes toward nursing play a large role in nurses' decision to migrate.

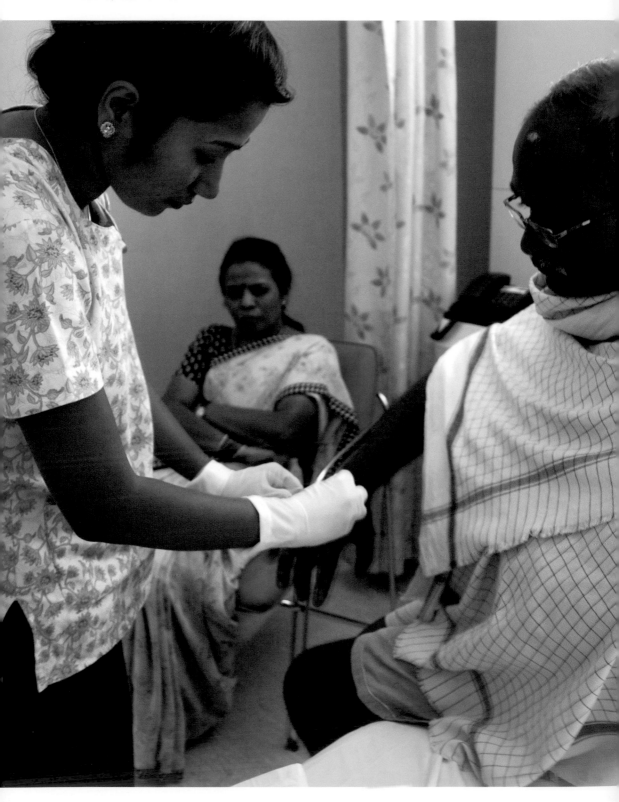

Young nurses were particularly eager to leave, as were those with a Bachelor's of Nursing rather than General Nursing qualifications. Nurses working in private employment were far more likely to want to migrate than nurses in government institutions, where pay and working conditions are somewhat better. This latter group was also more apprehensive about being able to cope with conditions abroad.

Many nurses felt it was impossible to fulfil the ideals of the profession in India and were willing to migrate to do so. The question of upward mobility also came up frequently, especially among middle and upper caste nurses who felt that government measures to promote opportunities for people from lower castes left them at a disadvantage. Thomas concluded: "To encourage more nurses to stay in India, government must allow nurses to practise. It is a shocking reality that of all categories of nurses, only the 'Community Health Worker' (who has a much lower level of knowledge and skill than the GNM or BSc (Nursing) or MSc (Nursing) has the legal right in India to prescribe medicines and provide treatment to patients. If nurses with higher-level qualifications are allowed to practise (of course, within clearly defined guidelines), then some of the most dynamic of them would see the scope for increasing their incomes as well as their social status while living in India, and this would have a positive effect on the entire nursing community in India."

Increase in pay scales is often suggested as a possible solution. However, the truth is that international wages differentials are so large that there is really not much scope for using higher wages as an incentive.

Philomina Thomas, Nursing Sister, All India Institute of Medical Sciences.

Stories of Nurse Migration

Caribbean Nurse Migration

In 1966, Annette Dear (née Smith), RN, set off from Trinidad to study nursing in the UK. Her career took her from England to Scotland to Canada and finally to Barbados. She talked to us about how each of these moves furthered her career as a nurse, about how she was received in different communities, and about what makes a place feel like 'home'.

I was born in Trinidad and became interested in nursing at about 12 when my brother was in hospital after a bicycle accident. I would visit him every day at lunch time, watch how the nurses looked after him, and help out because they were very short-staffed.

It would have been possible to study nursing at home, but by 1964 when I was finishing up at St Joseph's convent, my sister was studying in England and I really wanted to get away from home. In those days we were all part of the Commonwealth and could study in England without any problems.

I applied to many hospitals and my first acceptance came from Harefield Hospital in Middlesex. Some hospitals did not accept West Indian applicants to do the State Registered Nurse (SRN) programme. They took them to do the State Enrolled Nurse (SEN) programme, but SENs would only be qualified as nursing assistants back in the West Indies. I was accepted into the SRN programme.

So in May 1966, at the age of 19, I left for England. My sister warned that it would be a change: everyone was white, the food was bland, and it was cold.

All student nurses had to live in the residence at Harefield Hospital. There were only two British girls in the class. Others were from Singapore, other parts of the West Indies, Nigeria, Tanzania.

Our preliminary training session lasted three months, after which we went onto the wards. We had a second or third year nurse with us all the time showing us what to do. We got the lowly jobs like cleaning bedpans and dentures.

On our days off we would get together and walk around the countryside.

The only black people in Harefield at that time were people working at the hospital. Everyone knew we were nurses and, even though racism was strong, they treated us with respect because they knew that if anything happened to them, they would need our help.

By the third year we were involved in training new arrivals and preparing for our big exam, the General Nursing Council Exam, to become a State Registered Nurse. Most of us chose to specialise in obstetrics as we could complete that at Harefield.

I passed and worked in the cardiothoracic ward at Harefield as a staff nurse. But few of us were content to stop there. We wanted new challenges. The British girls went on to the Air Force, others moved on to hospitals elsewhere. Two stayed on as sisters at Harefield. I chose to specialise in midwifery and went to train at Craigtoun Maternity Hospital in Saint Andrews in Fife, Scotland. I then spent some time in London doing private duty nursing at the National Heart Hospital, where I gained experience with pediatric heart operations.

In the summer of 1973, I heard that the Canadian embassy officials were recruiting British trained midwives for hospitals in Toronto and Montreal. I met their criteria and was accepted as a candidate. Montreal had a certain mystique because a neighbour of mine in Trinidad had just been deported for taking part in a black student sit-in at Concordia University (Ann Cools, now a Canadian Senator, was also involved). I was very curious to see the place that had made such a quiet boy so radical!

The Royal Victoria Hospital has a large obstetrical unit and was within walking distance from McGill University, so I expressed my interest in working there, despite the fact that I would have to acquire a working knowledge of the French

The class at Harefield Hospital at the start of their training in 1966. Five left after the first year. Annette Dear (née Smith) is fourth from the right.

language within a year in order to keep practising. The Canadian hospitals were offering a much higher salary than we could have dreamed of getting in England. I also liked the prospect of being closer to Trinidad. From Dorval airport in Montreal, I took a taxi directly to the hospital and was provided accommodations until I found an apartment nearby.

I worked first in the normal nursery and then was offered a position in the Neonatal Intensive Care Unit (NICU). I stayed at the Royal Victoria Hospital for 14 years, eventually becoming Assistant Head Nurse in the NICU. The team and the work kept me there. We had very strong leadership from the Director of the NICU, the nursing supervisor and the head nurse, and relationships based on respect and fun. Caring for premature babies is complex but also immensely rewarding.

At the Embassy in London, the Canadians told us we would automatically be granted landed immigrant status in Canada and could apply for citizenship after three years. I did so in 1978 because I didn't think I was going anywhere else. I had married Jack, who was up from Barbados studying film at Concordia University. Soon we had two sons and many friends. Montreal had become home.

When our sons started school, Jack wanted to go back to Barbados because he felt the primary and secondary education was much better than in Canada. He also thought it important that they see black people in high positions in society. I wasn't

ready to leave at that time, but it was a positive move for our family and after high school, my elder son returned to Montreal to study biochemistry at McGill. He has since completed medical school at The University of the West Indies (UWI) Mona Campus in Jamaica and is currently doing his residency in General Surgery at the Dalhousie University Hospitals in Nova Scotia, Canada.

In Barbados, I was in touch with a neonatologist involved in a new hospital and there was an opportunity for me to run the NICU once it opened. However that doctor bowed out of the project and I didn't pursue it further. I was also interested in opening a long-term care facility as there was a growing need and not much around. A nursing friend and I looked at various locations, but she decided to return to England. So I worked in the midwifery department of the Bayview Hospital until my career took an unexpected turn one night when the actress Claudette Colbert was admitted for a stroke. I was looking after her, and her caregiver offered me work as a private nurse. It was a very different kind of nursing, quite lonely at times. But she was a fascinating woman with some very good stories to tell. She passed away in 1996.

I've never regretted my decision to become a nurse and to travel. The friends I've made along the way are scattered all over the world, but we're still close. And with one son in Canada, I have strong connections to the place I still consider my home.

A Natural Inclination to Caring

Mavis Stewart, RGN, RM, MBE set off from Jamaica to the "Mother Country" in 1954 and built a rewarding and extensive career nursing in London, as a Registered Nurse, midwife and health visitor, amongst other roles. She gave us just some of her observations from her years of experience.

As a child and young woman, Mavis always liked the idea of being a nurse; she had a natural inclination to caring, and made it known that she wanted to go into nursing. At 16, she went to a private nursing school in Kingston and, when a friend told her that she was going to 'the Mother Country' to work, Mavis began to apply to hospitals in the UK, securing a place at Queen Mary's in East London. In mid-1950s Jamaica, post-war Britain was advertising for nurses and a powerful patriotism meant that many elected to travel from Jamaica to pursue careers in the UK.

Her parents didn't want her to go; they worried she would be lonely, she would never return and that she would encounter something, they told her, called "the colour bar".

"Finally they agreed. I was very excited, I wanted so much to do my nursing there and learn about the newest trends in nursing and medicine, to learn about diseases that were affecting our people, to learn about Aneurin Bevan's NHS. We read about this in Jamaica—this man who had invented this 'National Health Service', which was the envy of the world. And I wanted to be a part of this."

Mavis left Jamaica for London in 1954 to finish her nurse training. "I wanted to see the place that I had learnt so much about as a young girl. The land of Shakespeare and Dickens, and Oliver Goldsmith's "The Deserted Village"."

In September that year, she traveled by plane from Kingston to New Jersey, then by boat across the Atlantic to Southampton. She was 19 and, although others were making similar journeys, she traveled alone. She arrived in the evening, and made her way across London to Stratford.

"I thought everyone in England spoke like the people in the Diplomatic Corps or on the BBC World Service; I thought they were well spoken. When I got on the train, the 'tube', I said, "Good evening everybody." Because that's how I was brought up. A few of them looked at me over their papers but nobody answered and I thought, 'well, this is the Mother Country but I am not

going to like my cousins. They are not very friendly. I don't think I am going to like it here.'"

She was met by the 'Home Sister', who told her where to eat and where to go for her uniform the following morning. Joining others from all over the Commonwealth: nurses from the Caribbean, the Orient and South Africa; doctors from Canada and Nigeria, she settled in and started her training.

"Over time, I began to notice the difference in accents, and to realise that England did indeed have a class system. Different classes dealt with things in different ways. For example, in the East End of London, people would say 'I would like you to come to tea, nurse, to thank you for what you have done. If you tell us what dates you can come, it would be very nice to have you.'

When I first went to tea, my hostess brought a great big rice pudding, and I mean seriously big, and she said, 'I hear you people like rice, dear.' I'll never, never forget that. And I started to cry because what I saw was not the rice pudding: it was the maternal gesture to someone new to the UK and a long way from home.

With the middle classes things could be different. I remember I delivered a baby and mother said, 'Do come around and see me; we would love to see you.' So, one day, when I was off duty, I thought, 'I'll go and see them'. I didn't have my uniform on and they looked embarrassed. I said, 'Well you did invite me to come and see you.'

So she sat me in the kitchen. I said, 'I just popped in to say hello to you and the baby, so I won't stay.' And I realised that when some people say, 'do drop in' that it doesn't mean anything. And so I learned that the apparent diplomacy of the middle classes was different to the outspoken straightforwardness of the working classes. I learned a lot along the way.

I really enjoyed my nursing career. I enjoyed the camaraderie that we had in the nurses' home. I enjoyed learning about diseases and seeing that England led the way in finding a cure for TB, that diphtheria, whooping

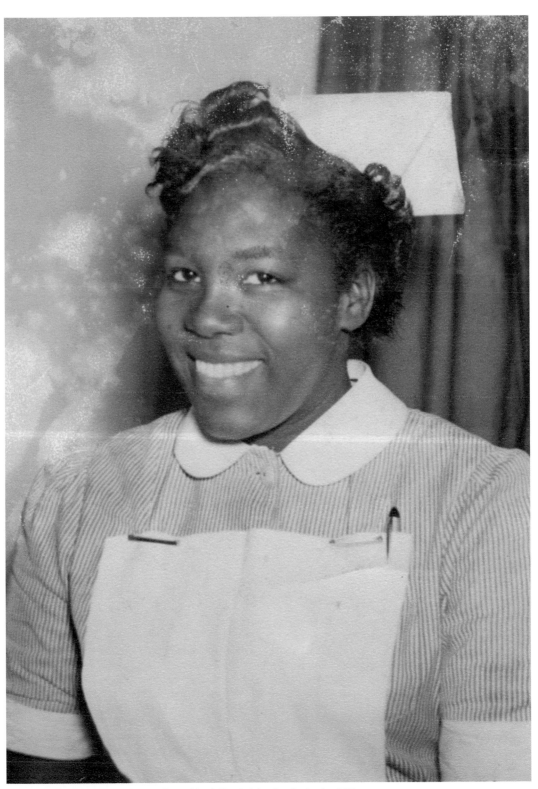

Mavis in uniform during her training at Queen Mary's Hospital, London, England, c 1955.

cough, tetanus and polio were not killers and immunisation was available. I noticed that the Health Service was looking at these things, and that made me want to stay even more. It was a very exciting time and, later on, when I was a nursing officer in the Health Service, people would come from all over the world to look at the NHS, with a view to modeling their own services on ours. We really were the envy of the world and I am proud to have been part of that.

I enjoyed delivering babies; I enjoyed the feeling of bringing life into the world and seeing fathers present at their child's delivery. We had a lot of home deliveries in those days.

And I was able to compare middle class women in labour with working class women, black women from the Caribbean with white women, and I observed as I went along how they behaved in labour. Black women would scream the whole place down and white working class women would say, 'It's his fault!' The middle class women would grunt and utter very, very controlled cries. The fathers began to play their part. During one delivery, a father was pushing along with his wife. I wished he'd leave the room. Healthy eating was becoming very much the order of the day: 'Here you are darling, have a dried banana.' And I thought, 'Darling is pushing. The contractions are becoming increasingly frequent. The birth is imminent. She doesn't want a dried banana! Clear off and make some tea!' What I actually said was, 'Would you mind making some tea please?.'

I used to get endless cups of tea lined up, but it was terrific and I still regard those times as a privilege and a memorable experience.

I was seeing and learning a lot about the whole question of medicine, and medicinal and nursing care. And I have never lost that interest to this day. I wanted to diversify my nursing so that I could see and learn everything that there was to learn.

I was introduced to my future husband by one of the dining room staff for the nurses in my training school. Don't forget that we had no families so we made friends with many different kinds of people—the porters and the hospital staff and the doctors. So I met my husband, and we became friends over the next couple of years. We began dating, and the rest, as they say, is history. We married in 1961 and we were married for nearly 47 years when he

passed away. He knew I loved nursing and he encouraged me to progress in my career, as I did him.

I noticed that the time that mothers stayed in hospital was becoming less—ten days rather than 14. There were a lot more home deliveries. There were few absent fathers and very few unmarried men and women. Those who were would still wear a ring because their husband 'was in the army or the navy'. It was that sort of era."

As a midwife, Mavis encountered many health visitors and it was this that encouraged her to train as one.

"That was very rewarding indeed. It was, I think, the highlight of my career. I really saw a whole cross-section of families. I began to learn about social deprivation, the class system, how schooling influenced where people lived, even more than when I was a midwife.

I saw the good, the bad and the ugly. I was able to see prejudice in the raw, because some people still didn't expect me to speak English, and they would make signs: 'CAN... I... HELP... YOU?' As I got older, I got bolder and sometimes I wouldn't say anything; I would look lost and watch them struggle. After a while I would say, 'Are you having trouble with the language? And here was I thinking that you were English?' I was very cheeky, and I think my humour helped a lot in my work.

The work of the health visitor was mostly about prevention. Don't forget that now we had immunisation and TB vaccinations. It was a very exciting time because our children were guaranteed healthier lives. Most mothers embraced the idea of immunisation but, for those who didn't, we would give them leaflets, tell them about the diseases, and explain that this was how they could protect their child. We would start off with good antenatal care. The midwife and health visitor would visit, and talk about things that would be provided for the care of mother and child. And so health promotion became a crucial part of how we worked. It was very exciting and Britain continued to influence other parts of the world.

Health visiting opened a whole new door for me. The most exciting part of it was seeing the new developments in the health service and watching the NHS grow. The new treatments for cancer, the exciting drugs that were developing—the established use of antibiotics and, of course, the Pill and the marvellous range of contraception that was becoming available. The excitement about the Health Service and its progress was always there, and it just got better and better. Doctors came from all over the world, very often Australia, South Africa, Canada, the United States. And they would bring their knowledge or come to learn from us.

As the Health Service grew, I noticed that the UK began to rely more on employing foreign labour. Although a lot of the Commonwealth countries were securing their independence, there were still many areas where Britain retained empirical interests, and so people would come and work here. Some would go back, some would stay but we could not manage to survive without this input."

Though retired, Mavis continues to work in health, using her extensive knowledge and experience in health promotion. "I continue to do some health teaching here and there and, because I am diabetic and I know that the Caribbean population is abnormally high in the incidence of diabetes, I would go anywhere I could to talk about diabetic health. Then I was asked to be the researcher and narrator on a film about healthy eating from a Caribbean perspective and I wrote some leaflets and made a video about healthy eating. Then I diagnosed my husband with prostate cancer; he lived for 14 years because of that early diagnosis. I became passionate about disease prevention. Although I am retired, I still have an interest in the Health Service. I still encourage people to work in it. I will see people and I will say, 'you have wonderful sensitive qualities, you'd make a marvellous nurse. Have you thought of that?'"

Mavis' passion and commitment to the NHS leads to frustrations with some of the change she is witnessing, often around an apparent lack of common sense.

"Nursing stations on wards for dementia patients should be sensibly located, not at the opposite end of the ward from the entrance; hygiene standards should not be lowered. Nurses shouldn't wear their uniforms out of the hospital; there should be a place for them to change before ward work starts, and they should have time to change their clothes and shoes as part of their paid working day. And nurses should look like nurses in uniforms that signify cleanliness and efficiency. The nursing shortage means that we could be in danger of compromise; one of the problems is around language. The ability for all hospital staff to communicate clearly is essential and employing nurses who are not able to use the language properly of the country in which they work brings huge problems."

"The National Health Service is something of which we should be proud, though I know there are areas of it that are of concern. We need to look at an NHS that maintains a responsibility and duty of care to provide for its community a good healthcare system that is up to date, progressive and successful, with ongoing research to make it even better and more progressive. I think that many people take it for granted; unless you really have traveled the road that I have, you don't realise what a special service we have. It may not be able to remain the same—much has changed universally—but the ideology must be respected."

"I say 'use it, but don't abuse it'. My work in health visiting showed me the amount of social deprivation in this country. Pretty well on my arrival from Jamaica, I noticed that there is a rigid class system in operation. As my career developed, I recognised that this impacts on the health of the poorest. I was able to take my knowledge and turn it into my most recent work in promoting healthy eating and lifestyle."

"I tell people not to rely on the Health Service to do the preventive part of the work, so that they can really get on with the care, the management of disease. We can work together towards better care. Let's look at the ways in which we as individuals can help the Health Service to ensure that it is there for the really necessary cases. We can eat healthily. We can remain fit and take exercise. We can help ourselves."

Nurse probationers with a Queen's Nurse in Bermuda, 1909. "After making more or less elaborate preparation for three years' sojourn abroad, the day arrived when I must leave Old England behind and sail for these Islands of Bermuda, knowing little about them or the work awaiting me there, and nothing at all about sea voyages."

"It was quite early one morning when we sighted St David's Lighthouse on one of the Bermuda Islands. We sailed slowly round the dangerous reefs to the entrance to the harbour... then a tug boat came for us and with it the Hon Secretary of the Bermuda Nursing Association, who talked to me of my new work as we steamed along through the small islands dotted about the harbour.

"The nurses had been left to themselves for many months and did not appreciate the changes I found it necessary to make. The work is not done in the orthodox way, still the plan adopted seems to work very well on the whole. The cooking is also done by the nurses, each taking a week in turn... the work in the Home and on the district is often very acute and interesting."[54]

A Sojourn Abroad

Tarsha Rook, RN, completed her nursing training in Adelaide, Australia before moving to the UK in 1997. She recently returned home and described how different health systems affect nursing care.

"Australia is very much a nation that likes to travel before settling, and many Australian nurses are geared up to do this once they finish university. One of the reasons I chose nursing was precisely because of the travel possibilities.

Moving to the UK was a relatively easy move. I applied for my 'right of abode' through my English mother, which allowed me to live and work in the UK, as long as my passport was valid. I didn't plan to work as a nurse immediately, but I would have been so badly paid doing anything else, I started work as an agency nurse.

I did all my fact-finding, including the rules and regulations I had to comply with in order to come to the UK to work, through the UKCC (United Kingdom Central Council for Nursing, Midwifery, and Health Visiting), though I think it is harder now to comply with all the UK regulations."[55]

After her stint in the UK, Tarsha found returning to Australia was straightforward. "For me it was easy to find work, as Australia is very short of experienced nurses and, unlike the UK, they have relaxed the registration rules. I used to work between countries and would regularly return home to visit my parents. It was a big hassle to re-register every year with the nurse's board in Australia—I would have to bring references and all my pay slips to prove my hours and my pay-rate. Now, although each state is different, all I have to do is confirm that I have worked as a nurse in the last five years, and where."

"The move between countries was fascinating—culturally, surprisingly different despite the language being the same. I found the NHS a very different system to Medicare in Australia, which is a more private, insurance-based system. This allows more money in the system and shorter waiting times. I loved working in the UK, but found the lack of staffing and facilities in some hospitals frustrating. The high use, and high pay, of agency nurses was wonderful for me while I travelled but, once settled into a permanent position in the NHS, it was frustrating to see hospital staffing budgets spent this way."

"From nursing, I wanted the 'people' contact and to be a part of the helping ethos; I also liked the idea of the multitude of career paths it offered. My nursing career has been diverse and has given me freedom to work and travel; it is now giving me the opportunity to work and have a family. I am amazed at how much more flexible nursing has become to keep the nurses in the profession. My current job as a funding facilitator in a 120-bed medium care nursing home is desk-based, and allows me the part-time hours I need as the mother of two children."

Tarsha believes that the challenges facing nursing are around pay levels and flexibility. "The pay needs to increase and the work/life balance to become more flexible. Nursing as a profession is losing staff through poor pay and rigid shift work. I think there is an uncapped mid-30s market of female nurses who have been, 'out' having children, and have lost confidence and need retraining. Sadly, I can earn more as a waitress than I can as a GP practice nurse. It can be impossible to juggle kids with early or late night shifts and school holidays; flexible contracts would help to balance this."

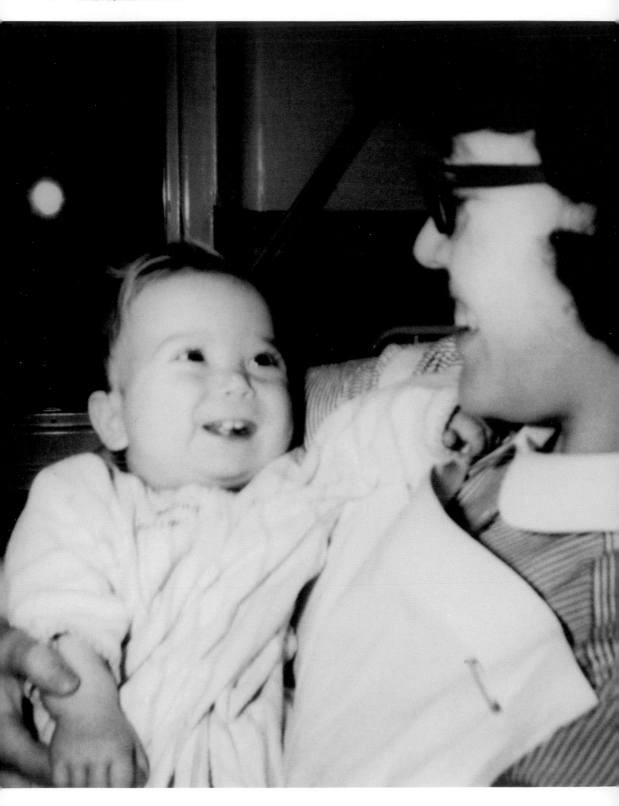

Christine Hancock in her second year as a student nurse, King's, London, England.

An International Perspective

Christine Hancock, RN, was President of the International Council of Nurses for four years and General Secretary of the Royal College of Nursing for 12. She has visited all parts of the world and writes here about the basic commonalities she found in nurses and the challenges they face. In 2009, Christine formed C3 Collaborating for Health a new, not-for-profit organisation based in London which works globally to eradicate preventable chronic diseases.

Christine trained at King's College London, becoming Ward Sister at London's National Heart Hospital and later Director of Nursing for Bloomsbury, an area of London that includes some of the city's largest hospitals. More recently, she was Chief Executive of Waltham Forest Health Authority.

She had a high profile in the 12 years she was General Secretary of the Royal College of Nursing (RCN). Under her leadership nurses chose to join the RCN in increasing numbers making it the fastest growing trade union in the UK. She led the RCN to work honestly but critically with changing governments and secured for nurses a voice that was listened to.

During Christine's presidency of the ICN, she visited 50, mostly low income, countries, meeting nurses and seeing health services. About half those countries were in Europe, including Eastern Europe, five Latin American countries, six African countries, Thailand, Japan, Lebanon, Dubai and more.

"One of the strongest impressions at the end of the four years was the commonality of nursing across the world, which might be one reason why migration is the phenomenon in nursing that it is. But, I also witnessed the commonality of the problems that nurses face. Three things stood out for me around the globe:
1. Relative pay. For example nurses in Luxembourg are paid better than anywhere else in Europe, and nurses pour in from France, Germany and Belgium to work there because the salaries are so high. But they are not paid as well as postmen in Luxembourg. So, despite the fact that they are incredibly well paid, they are actually frustrated and devalued.
2. A feeling that there aren't enough of you to do the work that needs to be done; I think this is as true in California as it is in Uganda, even though California has a far greater proportion of nurses to patients. I think it is about not being able to control and influence your workload. This leads to the third point.
3. Nurses everywhere do not have a strong enough voice in policy: within their work place (which is probably most important) but also within government and national policy. My belief is that this is overwhelmingly about gender, but it is a complex pathway and what to do about it is very challenging. One of the very interesting things is the aggression, sometimes from nurses themselves, towards nurses being better educated. It is not about intelligence; it is more that nursing comes from a very practical tradition. Nurses have a very pragmatic way of thinking about what they do and how they do it, rather than trying to analyse their actions and roles. But other practical roles are also academically based (engineers, architects and indeed medicine). I know of no evidence that says if you're better educated you're less caring or less good with your hands.

One of the things that I say to nurses is that they need the support of physicians and patients/the public: 'there must be one or two supportive physicians in your country; you have to find them and get them to help speak on your behalf'.

Worldwide, the environments in which nurses are working are very different, from remarkable affluence to marked poverty, from natural disasters to war zones. One of my most moving experiences has been meeting nurses who have had to flee their country. Or nurses who had come to the UK to escape regimes in Latin America. Or nurses in Africa dealing with AIDS, both as nurses and as patients. I met staff in Eastern Croatia who spent six weeks in a basement while the attackers bombarded them, whose patients were then apparently taken to the Red Cross, but who were in fact executed.

There is also a growing disparity in the quality and availability of care within countries. In Nairobi, I visited a well-run, clean, quiet public hospital and went round a ward of 30 beds in which 95 patients were being cared for: a bed and two mattresses in single rooms, two patients in every bed. I said to the Director, "How can you do your job?" She said, "What can we do Christine? People are so ill; we can't turn them away." In the same city, I visited a top of the range private hospital, probably better than anything in many rich countries in terms of equipment and facilities. This disparity is about the 'haves' and the 'have-nots'. Countries aren't going to be able to sustain that kind of disparity when everybody has access to the television and the internet, and can see what is happening and what is possible. This also applies to nurses, because it is difficult not to take the opportunity of going to work for the top of the range hospital, once the choice is evident.

Some of the most outstanding nurses in the poorest countries have been those working in communities. One of the people that made the biggest impact on me was a well-educated, public health nurse in Uganda. She was running a health facility with few beds; it was poor. The first thing she showed me was the incinerator; the second, the water pump. She was also collecting some statistics about vaccinations. With no information technology (IT), she was recording them on a board. She had a very systematic approach in trying to vaccinate and I was so impressed with what she was doing. She was like a one-woman 'Health Maintenance Organisation' (HMO). And that wasn't unique. It was clearly to do with her personal beliefs; being that well educated she could have been working somewhere else, and I doubt that she was that well paid.

There are different types of nurse working in different roles. There is the nurse who enjoys the buzz of critical emergency care. There is the type of nurse that wants the continuity of relationships. A challenge of modern nursing is that one of the motivations for going into nursing is to look after people, while the whole trend of hospital care is that patient stays are short. As a nurse this means that you are caring for people you hardly know. Which is quite a different scenario from, say, the 1950s when people stayed in bed for six weeks after a heart attack and you looked after them constantly, and got to know them well.

Some of the things I feel strongly about are the same things that Florence Nightingale believed passionately that nurses should be responsible for: properly managed ventilation, nutritious food and cleanliness. Over the years these roles and responsibilities have been taken away from nurses as a fundamental part of looking after patients.

When I was Director of Nursing in Bloomsbury based in University College Hospital (UCH), in the early 1980s, it was the time of privatisation of the cleaning services. I persuaded our Chairman (who was a GP) that we should only put out to tender our office and outpatient services, not our cleaning services, which I believed were an integral part of caring for patients. The administrative staff said I had ruined the contract and, from a financial perspective, they were probably right. But cleaning and food: they are fundamental to patient recovery. UCH was one of the last hospitals where the ward sisters still served the meals. Having a responsibility for seeing what people eat is an essential part of care. There has been a lot of work over the years that tells us that post-surgical patients do not always get enough protein to assist their wounds to heal. As a patient, food and cleanliness are all a part of care and nurturing.

Nursing is not an easy profession, and nurses have lost what used to be informal 'counselling', or peer support. When I trained, the age of majority was 21, so the hospital was, in a sense, our guardian. We were all between 18 and 21 and we all lived in—and living in meant support. I can remember we talked through with each other our first death, or a resuscitation that didn't work. Nobody would have called that counselling, but it was good to reflect on a tough experience. Now lots of nurses are married, or they travel, or they are looking after their kids. They don't necessarily need formal counselling as much as an opportunity to debrief, to talk things through.

To some extent, nursing is a constant challenge—people do die, things do go wrong— but, in today's culture of carefully managed systems and structures, we haven't replaced what used to be an informal opportunity for people to talk about difficult things."

Christine Hancock, early years as General Secretary of the RCN.

One of the strongest impressions at the end of my four years as President of the International Council of Nursing (ICN) was the commonality of nursing across the world... but I also witnessed the commonality of the problems that nurses face.

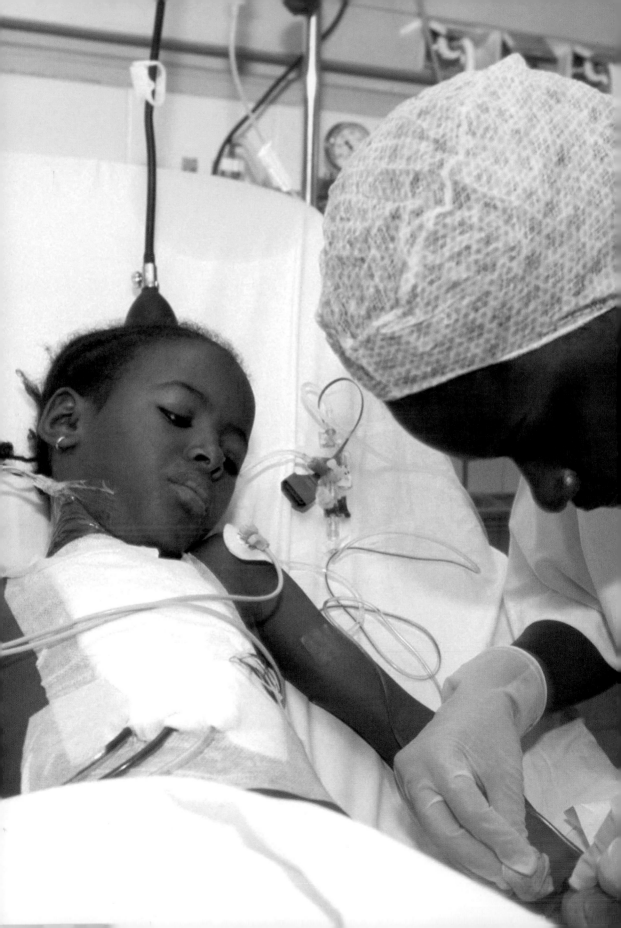

3
The
Workplace:
Hospital,
Home and
Beyond

The Workplace: Hospital, Home and Beyond

Nurses work everywhere from academic hospitals to patients' homes to field hospitals in war and disaster zones. This Chapter looks at nursing practice in these different environments. Over half of nurses in many countries work in hospitals. We trace how healthcare design is evolving with new knowledge on the impact of the physical environment on patient outcomes and staff satisfaction. The Nightingale ward may be giving way to private rooms, but her preoccupation with light, air and quiet retains a central importance. Nurses know better than anyone what makes hospitals function smoothly but have had little opportunity to influence their design. This may be changing. We asked nurses in one major centre to describe how they made themselves heard in the redevelopment of their hospital.

Home and community care are expanding quickly and gaining respect after years of hospital dominance. A Queen's Nurse from the UK talks about a venerable nursing role that is now making a comeback. We also find out about pioneering work in tele-nursing that is increasing access to home care.

The field hospitals of war zones and mobile clinics of relief efforts are enormously challenging workplaces. Nurses who take on these assignments are driven to help people in their time of greatest need and do what they can to uphold human rights. We hear from Carol Etherington, an American nurse who has led programmes to help communities cope during war and natural disaster at home and abroad, and from Ghislaine Télémaque, who divides her time between nursing in the First Nations and Inuit communities of Québec's far north and humanitarian missions with international agencies.

PREVIOUS PAGES A nurse at the intensive care unit at Le Dantec Hospital, Dakar, 1999.

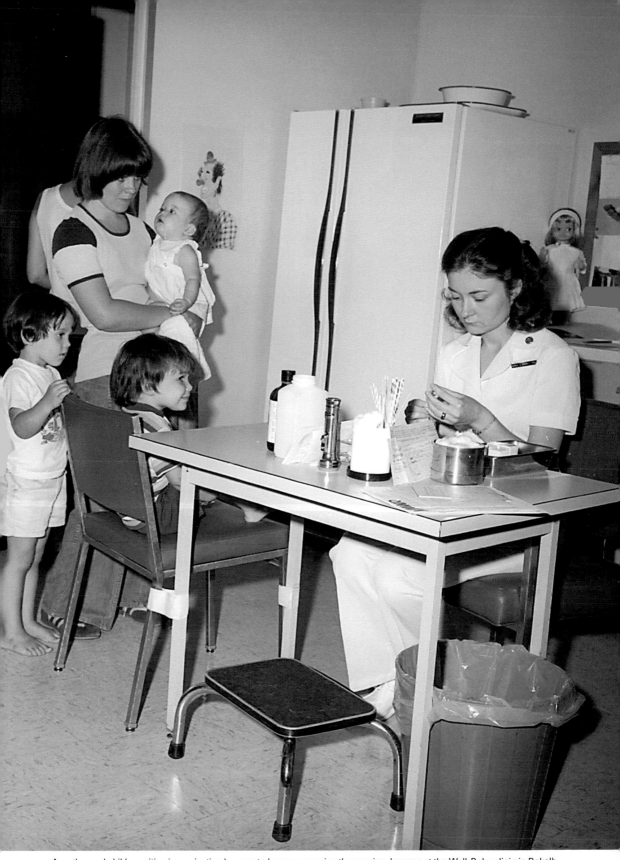

A mother and child, awaiting immunisation by a seated nurse preparing the vaccine dosages at the Well-Baby clinic in Dekalb County, Georgia, USA, 1977.

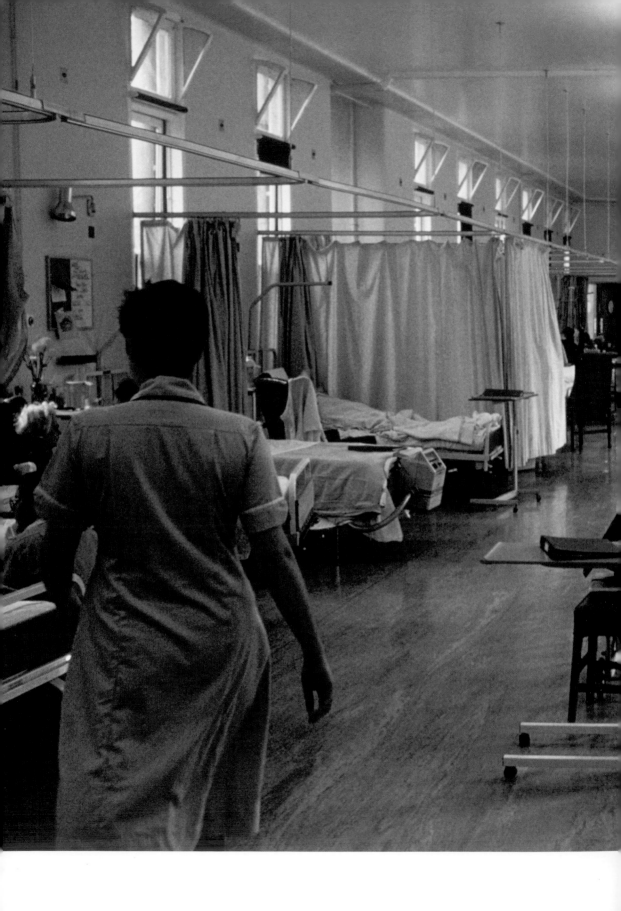

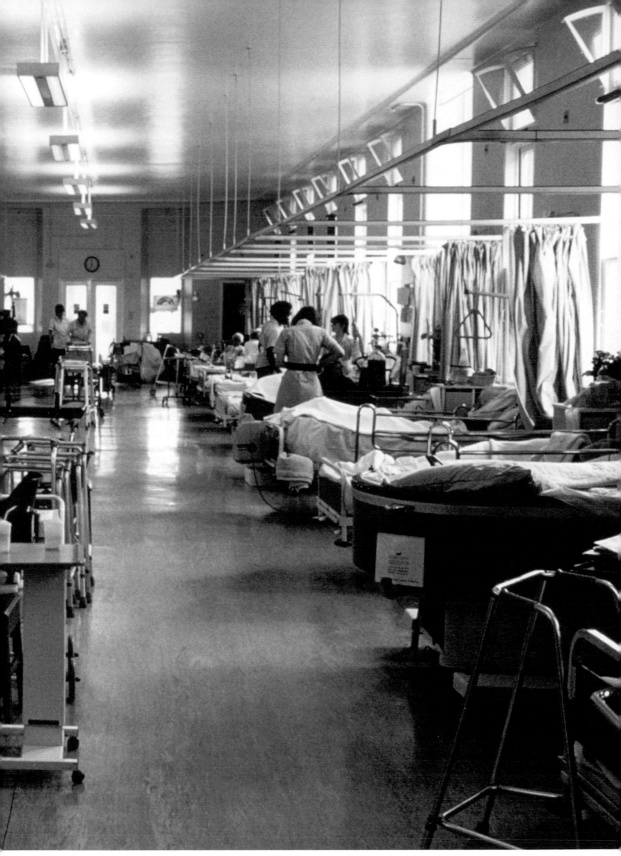

The Matthew Whiting Ward at King's College Hospital, London, England.

Rinkai Hospital, Tokyo, Japan.

The Hospital

The role and nature of the hospital is changing along with changes in the delivery of care. The economic case for large hospitals is constantly under scrutiny, as is their environmental sustainability; in some places, the hospital of the future has started to look less like the hospital as we know it.

There is a great deal to be said about the ways in which a well-designed building is key to the way that care is given. Design has often been focused firstly on the patient; however, a great deal of what is good for patients is good for staff and visitors too. Successful healthcare building design can support those providing care, and create an environment in which access to services for patients is made easier. The key characteristics of design apply as much to smaller community health buildings as to huge super-hospitals, and this section looks at those characteristics, with nurses in mind.

OPPOSITE The Arches, in Belfast, Northern Ireland, one of three new Community Treatment and Care Centres designed to provide a range of health and social care services under one roof. Penoyre and Prasad with Todd Architects, 2005.

Fundamentals of Healthcare Design

Today, nurses, clinicians and medical planners, building commissioners and managers, architects and designers the world over know that it is possible to create robust buildings to clinical standards that provide a humane environment for care. In the UK, the Commission for Architecture and the Built Environment (CABE) has done a great deal of work setting out key principles of healthcare design, working with a wide range of organisations to promote the value of commissioning and designing high quality healthcare buildings.[1] These principles are no longer always seen as the softer luxuries, but as sensible approaches to staff and patient care:

+ Environments that underline not undermine the care that takes place inside them.

+ Therapeutic, healing environments that contribute to calm in potentially anxious situations, and therefore support healing.

+ Good integrated design—hospitals and smaller healthcare buildings are major pieces of our urban realm, and should make a positive contribution.

+ Well-organised space with a clear plan.

+ Wayfinding that supports care rather than creates additional anxiety with good circulation and waiting areas.

+ An environment that maximises natural light and ventilation.

+ Environments that offer privacy, dignity and support patient safety.

+ Good quality reception areas and a well-considered 'welcome'.

+ Spaces that are easily managed and maintained and are therefore clean, tidy, and communicate calm, efficient care.

+ Sufficient, appropriate storage: a place for everything and everything in its place.

+ Environments that appropriately embrace flexibility, adaptability and future-proofing.

+ Well-considered corridors, both in terms of quantity and quality.

+ Environments that address security (for staff, visitors and patients).

+ High quality gardens, outdoor spaces, or courtyards.

+ High quality and environmentally sensitive approach to design, materials and finishes, construction and management.

+ Places for staff to rest and relax.

+ An accessible and inclusive design approach that says to all patients and staff that "this healthcare is for me".

... the potential power of buildings to inspire a positive emotional response and foster mental well-being among patients and their families cannot be denied. A run-down hospital is hardly the best setting for helping people to face disease positively, gain control over their fears, and reorganise their lives.[2]

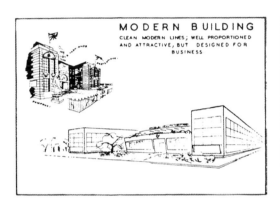

MODERN BUILDING
CLEAN MODERN LINES; WELL PROPORTIONED AND ATTRACTIVE, BUT DESIGNED FOR BUSINESS

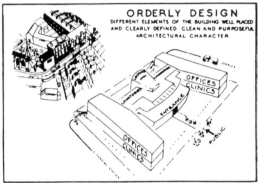

ORDERLY DESIGN
DIFFERENT ELEMENTS OF THE BUILDING WELL PLACED AND CLEARLY DEFINED CLEAN AND PURPOSEFUL ARCHITECTURAL CHARACTER

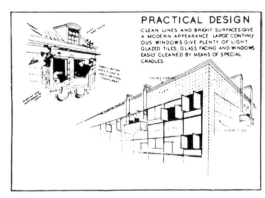

PRACTICAL DESIGN
CLEAN LINES AND BRIGHT SURFACES GIVE A MODERN APPEARANCE. LARGE CONTINUOUS WINDOWS GIVE PLENTY OF LIGHT GLAZED TILES, GLASS FACING AND WINDOWS EASILY CLEANED BY MEANS OF SPECIAL CRADLES.

CHEERFUL ATMOSPHERE
ENTRANCE HALL FLOODED WITH LIGHT THROUGH WALL OF GLASS BRICKS CLEAN SURFACES AND BRIGHT COLOURS PRODUCE CHEERFUL EFFECT AIR OF EFFICIENCY GIVES CONFIDENCE TO THE PATIENTS

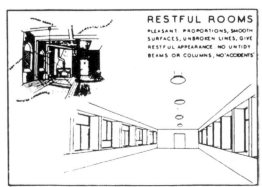

RESTFUL ROOMS
PLEASANT PROPORTIONS, SMOOTH SURFACES, UNBROKEN LINES, GIVE RESTFUL APPEARANCE. NO UNTIDY BEAMS OR COLUMNS, NO 'ACCIDENTS'

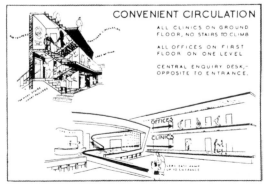

CONVENIENT CIRCULATION
ALL CLINICS ON GROUND FLOOR, NO STAIRS TO CLIMB

ALL OFFICES ON FIRST FLOOR ON ONE LEVEL

CENTRAL ENQUIRY DESK,- OPPOSITE TO ENTRANCE.

More than 70 years ago, architect Berthold Lubetkin's Finsbury Health Centre in London, 1938, demonstrated the principles of creating a well-designed healing environment that we know so well today. These panels were created for a public exhibition to illustrate how the design of the building would help to support the health and well-being of the local community it was to serve.[3]

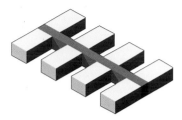

Linked pavilion or 'finger' plan. Still commonly used. The pavilions often have clinical spaces on lower levels with wards above.

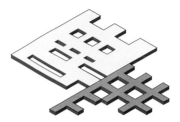

Low-rise multi-courtyard or 'checkerboard'. Offers more of a human scale than many high-rise hospitals; often seen in less urban sites or smaller hospitals.

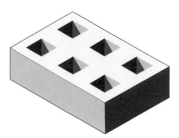

Monoblock. The lightwells offer a way of creating, for example, an atrium, though they may not benefit the lower floors.

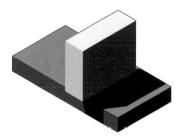

Podium and slab or tower. Wards are generally in the tower, with the clinical and technical areas in the slab.

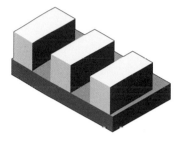

Podium with two or more towers or blocks. Similar to the 'podium and slab or tower', but likely to require a larger site.

Street. The attraction of this type of hospital is its logical layout that makes it easier to navigate around.

Atrium/galleria. A way of introducing natural light into a hospital building.

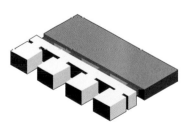

Unbundled. Diagnostic and treatment functions are separated from the nursing functions, along shared circulation down the centre of the hospital building.

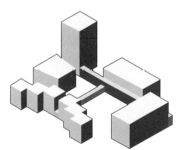

Campus. Individual buildings built on one hospital site, sometimes with enclosed circulation.

Hospital Typologies

These drawings show the ways in which the main different types of hospital we know today are arranged—their general size and scale (for example, whether they are single or multi-storey), the way that their different components are arranged to make the shape of the hospital, and the relationship between indoor and outdoor space. Hospitals may be a combination of the different arrangements.[4]

OPPOSITE ACAD (Ambulatory Diagnostic and Treatment Centre), Central Middlesex Hospital, by Avanti.

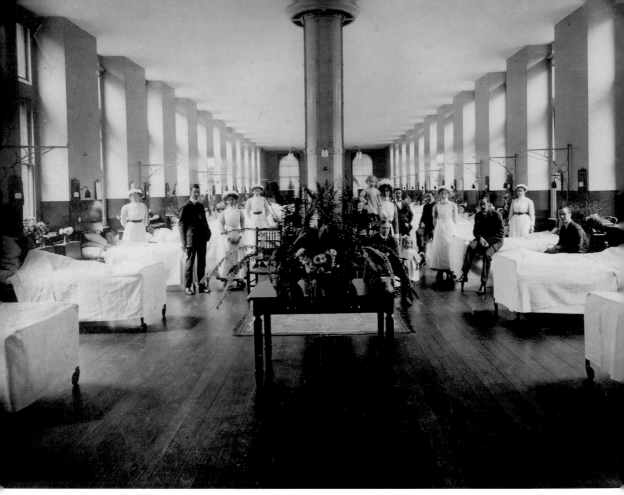

The Victoria Ward at St Thomas' Hospital, London, c 1900.

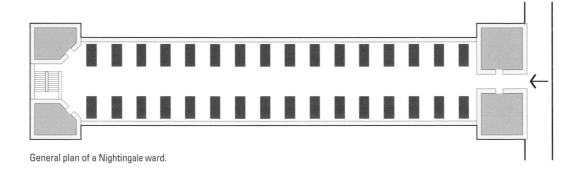

General plan of a Nightingale ward.

What is a Nightingale Ward?
... generally comprised 32 beds arranged in two rows at right angles to the windows, giving economy of staff movement with ease of supervision. Comparatively high standards of hygiene were achieved by high ceilings and good cross-ventilation, with a floor area per bed of about 100 square feet. Sanitary facilities were sited centrally or to one end and, together with a ward kitchen and an office, they comprised the whole of the ancillary rooms that were considered necessary.[8]

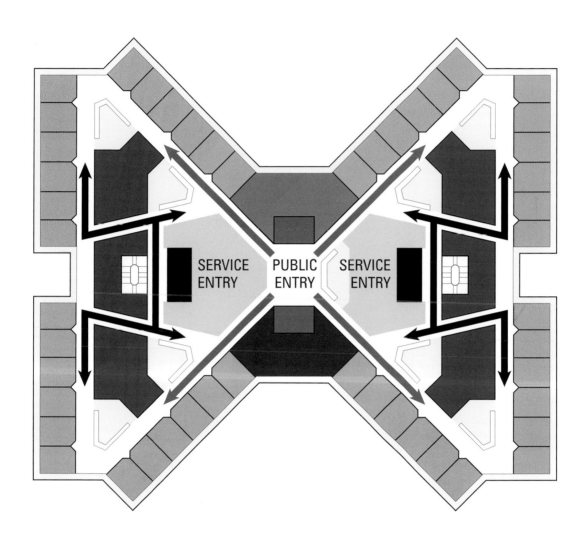

Modern Ward Design
One of the configurations proposed to the McGill University
Health Centre for its pediatric inpatient units. Concept study
by Ibghy/Yelle Maille Architects, collaborative consultant
Perkins and Will.

- Public circulation
- Service circulation
- Patient rooms
- Staff work area
- Physician and teaching area
- Family/Siblings
- Child Life
- Support services

The ground floor reception area at the Breast Care Centre, St Bartholomew's Hospital, London, by Greenhill Jenner Architects. The artwork on the wall is DJ Simpson's *Check, Double Check*.

Improving Patient Well-being

There is a large and increasing body of evidence that readily demonstrates how well-designed healthcare environments contribute to high quality care.[9] However there are many routes to success. The evaluation of healthcare buildings once they have opened is crucial, as is finding creative ways of using the knowledge and experience of building users (nurses, clinicians, other staff, patients and their visitors). Add to this an extensive bank of knowledge and professional expertise amongst all those—including nurses—involved in planning, designing, constructing and managing our healthcare estate and we have at our disposal a vast body of knowledge that can and should be brought to bear. Professional skills, training and experience as well as common sense count for a great deal in the design of a hospital.

"There is a growing awareness internationally among healthcare administrators and medical professionals of the need to create functional environments that also have patient-centred or supportive characteristics that help patients cope with the stress that accompanies illness. The key factor motivating awareness of facility design has been mounting scientific evidence that environmental characteristics influence patient health outcomes. Many studies have shown that well-designed environments can, for instance, reduce anxiety, lower blood pressure, and lessen pain. Conversely, research has linked poor design—or psychosocially unsupportive surroundings—to negative effects such as higher occurrence of delirium, elevated depression, greater need for pain drugs, and in certain situations longer hospital stays."[10]

OPPOSITE Basel University Hospital; original building completed in 1945, refurbishment and extension by Sylvia Gmür Livio Vacchini, 2003.

Nurse and patient picking roses in the garden of Sydnope Hall, Matlock, England, 1943.

Nurse Knows Best

It is all in a good brief. The people who use buildings most know best how those buildings work; in this case, the nurses. Investigations into the design of our workplaces reveal that the impact of their design impacts on productivity, efficiency, and morale.[11] In healthcare, it is important to acknowledge that looking after staff well makes it easier for them to look after patients. Here, the value of well-managed consultation with the right people; nurses know from experience what elements of hospital design would make their job easier/more efficient/more pleasant and would therefore impact positively on the patient experience.

Nurses constantly see how the design of their working environment impacts on staff and patients and, in 2004, CABE's Healthy Hospitals Campaign asked nurses in England to talk about their workplaces, in this case, hospitals.[12] Overwhelmingly, nurses said that they knew a great deal about how the design of their workplace impacted on their ability to provide care, and therefore on their patients, and that they would like to be asked more for their input and opinion. "99 per cent of nurses believe that it is important for them to be consulted on decisions about the design of hospitals, rising to 100 per cent for nurses in a management position or higher. But over half of all nurses (52 per cent) think that they do not currently influence the design and management of hospital environments at all."[13]

A nurse holds an infant patient in the sun room of St Louis Children's hospital, c 1910.

It makes you happier to be working in a nice environment—pleasant view, sufficient daylight and the possibility of opening a window for fresh air.

Nurse, Bristol, 2004.[14]

The central atrium of Carlisle Health and Well-being Centre in Belfast, Northern Ireland, by Penoyre and Prasad with Todd Architects, 2007.

As part of the campaign, the impact of hospital design on the recruitment, retention and performance of nurses was examined, concluding that:

+ Well-designed healthcare buildings contribute to enhanced performance and motivation [of nurses].

+ Good design is a factor in nurses' choice of hospitals.

+ A focus on internal design should be a priority—in particular the organisation of space on wards, units, storage and lighting (both natural and artificial).

+ Nurses want to be consulted about design, believe they can play a positive role in improving the design aspects of the areas in which they work and that consultation should begin early in the process.15

Maggie's Centre, Dundee, Scotland, 2004, Frank Gehry.

I have been to two different hospitals—one where there is nothing but corridors and a mish-mash of things added on, and staff morale is low. There is another hospital close by which is well laid out and nicely designed and staff morale is much better.

Nurse, Bristol, 2004.[16]

The study illustrated that, if staff are looked after well, they can more easily look after their patients, with 48 per cent of nurses surveyed "agreeing strongly that working in a well-designed hospital would help them do their job better".[17]

A range of requirements was identified that would improve nurses' day-to-day working lives, including spaces (indoor and outdoor) for rest and relaxation away from patients; sufficient appropriate working space, including storage; good staff facilities (lockers, places to shower and change, canteens close to workspaces); good organisation of space so that collecting necessary supplies does not mean walking great distances; natural light and control of the immediate working environment (especially ventilation and temperature); and high quality, well-designed robust interior fixtures and fittings.

Nurses Make Themselves Heard in Hospital Design

The construction of a new hospital is an opportunity to put new design knowledge in action. At Montréal's McGill University Health Centre, we spoke to former Director of Nursing Valerie Shannon, Associate Director of Nursing Susan Drouin and Associate Director of the Planning Committee Imma Franco about how nurses came together to influence their future workplace.

Nurses may know best, but gaining a voice in the design process requires tremendous commitment and collaboration. Nursing leaders at the McGill University Health Centre (MUHC) in Montréal, Canada, saw a unique opportunity to influence their future workplace as the MUHC moved to consolidate the facilities of five hospitals and a major Research Institute into two campuses. The Montréal General Hospital will be redeveloped as the Mountain Campus, the second will be built from scratch in a former railyard called "The Glen". The redevelopment involves two main stages. The first, completed in 1997, was to bring the five hospitals under unified leadership. The second is to build the new facilities. The MUHC employs over 11,000 people, including 3,000 nurses, and trains some 2,500 health professionals each year.

The planning process has stretched over a decade and nurses have been involved in operational, strategic and functional planning from the start. This marks a sea change from earlier generations, when hospital planning was reserved for physicians, administrators and wealthy developers.

When the MUHC redevelopment was first discussed as a possibility, Val Shannon was Director of Nursing at the Montréal General Hospital and went on to be the first Director of Nursing at the MUHC. She and Directors of Nursing from the four other hospitals met regularly and lobbied to make sure that one of them (Lorine Besel from the Royal Victoria Hospital) would be part of the planning group for the new MUHC. Despite an inherently competitive relationship between Directors of Nursing, Shannon says they knew they had to pull together on this project that would profoundly affect all MUHC nurses for generations to come.

The challenge for nurses was to anticipate how they would work in a physical environment that bore little relation to the wards of their current hospitals. In the early planning stages, nurses from each hospital site came together at periodic retreats over a year and a half to develop a vision of what they wanted the practice of nursing to look like in the physical entity that would be developed. They arrived at a vision of family-centered care and collaborative work, and this provided a common goal that nurses could rally around and work towards together.

Susan Drouin, Associate Director of Nursing in the Women's Health Mission at the MUHC, is a clinical advisor on one of the planning committees in the adult sector of the redevelopment. She has spent considerable time looking for ideal designs for the anticipated in-patient rooms in the new and renovated hospitals. The first round of consultations focused on the principles that should guide design: patient safety was a major issue, as was nurse effectiveness. Drouin and Patricia O'Connor, who is now Director of Nursing at the MUHC, then visited hospitals across the US to see what types of structure and technology could really make a difference on these two measures.

All modern hospitals in North America are moving to single patient rooms in response to patient requirements and research on healing environments. Single rooms require nurses to work differently. But there are so many benefits in terms of greater patient satisfaction and better outcomes, shorter length of stay, and reductions in medication errors, that nurses at the MUHC generally support the shift.

The pod of 12 individual rooms was adopted as the basis for the floor plan. Each pod would have space for small nursing stations for charting and consultations, moving nurses out of the central nursing station, which would become an administrative hub used by a large variety of health professionals involved in care.

The MUHC planners came up with room designs that responded to needs identified by clinical advisors. Individual patient rooms comprised three zones: the caregiver zone,

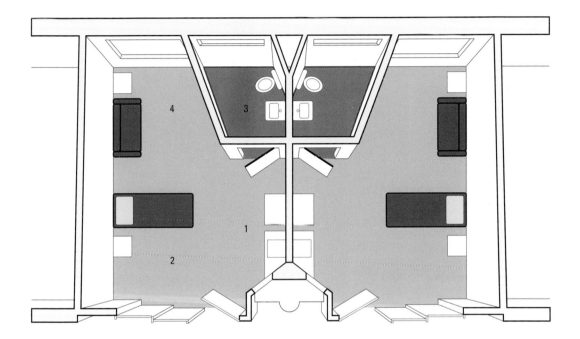

equipped with a sink, cupboards and counter, the patient zone and the family zone. "At the bedside," said Imma Franco, Associate Director of Planning for the MUHC since 1999, "what nurses want is to have all the tools they need around them. If a design facilitates this, they will approve."

Nurses at the MUHC today are excited, if a little nervous, about what the future has in store. But most of all, they are pleased at the new respect for nurses' needs, concerns, and knowledge about what can make a unit work better.

Nurses are seen as a finite resource and people understand we have to be employed in the most effective way possible.

Susan Drouin, Associate Director of Nursing in the Women's Health Mission, McGill University Health Centre.

Zones of Use in New Patient Rooms at the MUHC

1 Clinical zone for handwashing, a writing surface, a place for unit dose medications, sharps disposal, glove box, wastebasket and possibly a computer station.
2 Zone of the patient and the bed.
3 Hygiene zone that includes the patient's toilet.
4 Zone for the family. The typical family amenities include decent seating for more than one visitor and a recliner or sleeping couch.

The spacious waiting room at Kentish Town Health Centre, 2009, by Allford Hall Monaghan Morris Architects.

Results: Happier Nurses and Better Care

Kentish Town Health Centre

Mark Johnstone is Practice Nurse at Kentish Town Health Centre in north London. He comments: "Working at the Kentish Town Health Centre has provided a breath of fresh air in more ways than one—the wonderful naturally ventilated room allows me to simply open the door on a deck outside my consulting room—great when the sun shines. Also the airy and spacious waiting room with its own garden has led to a dramatic drop in the tension for those waiting—we have only had one aggressive incident in nine months—in our old premises we had around two each month."

Maggies's Centre, Fife, Scotland, 2006, by Zaha Hadid.

Maggie's Cancer Care Centre

Ruth McCabe is a trained nurse and managed a Hospice for 11 years before taking on the role as Centre Head at Maggie's Fife in November 2006. Ruth said: "It has been an incredible experience moving from the NHS to this environment. Three key differences stand out: the therapeutic space is specially designed; I have the time to spend with visitors, and I can make the best use of opportunities to reduce the isolation so frequently felt by people affected by cancer. My role is to let the tears flow and honour this level of emotion until the person can verbalise what is going on.

I find that the beautifully-designed centre helps to facilitate these open and honest conversations. The homely, warm and positive environment of a Maggie's Centre makes people feel at ease and open up as if they have just stepped into the home of a well-informed friend.

Some people come to Maggie's looking for transformation in their lives. Giving them a place to turn to which is surprising and thought provoking—even inspiring—will give them the setting and the benchmark of qualities they will need in themselves. Knowing there is a place to turn to which is special in itself makes you feel valued. My hope is that individuals and families will see the space as a sanctuary and will return again and again and use all the aspects of the programme suited to them. I believe Maggie's offers a truly holistic model of care and support to people with cancer and those closest to them, and that the stunning physical and healing environment greatly aids us to achieve our aim of empowering people to live with, through and beyond cancer."

District Nurse visiting flats in London, England, 1959. The nurse is originally from St Thomas, Jamaica.

Home and Community Care

In the public mind today, nurses are immediately associated with hospitals. As Dr Judith Shamian, CEO of the Victorian Order of Nurses (VON) in Canada states: "Everybody implicitly and explicitly believes that you have 'arrived' in the profession if you are in acute care." This was not always the case. A century ago, it was the District Nurse, arriving at the door with her black bag, or the VON nurse attending family births and deaths who captured the public imagination and imbued the profession with respect.

The second half of the twentieth century saw hospitals assume predominant positions in healthcare, a bias that was encased in the structure of public health systems in a number of countries. Regard for home and community nursing slipped. College and university training programmes paid scant attention to the specialty. "Oftentimes", comments Dr Shamian, "a nurse who might be interested in home and community care nursing will opt to go into the hospitals because they earn less in the community sector. Home care became very much production line nursing: You go into one home, do your work quickly and move to the next, with very little opportunity to support the family and provide education in health promotion as nurses did in earlier times."

But today the tide is turning once again and home and community nursing is assuming a much more important place in overall health system design, despite the fact that it is still not funded at the same level as hospital care. Most developed nations are facing an ageing population that wants to remain at home as long as possible, and die at home. "It will require a tremendous shift in how we deal with caregivers, volunteers and how we structure the healthcare system", Dr Shamian believes. And nurses will be leading the way.

Dr Shamian regards independence and flexibility as major draws for nurses coming into community and home care. "They are able to use their knowledge and judgement in a much broader way than they can in the hospital sector. So they can go into a home to look at someone's wound dressing, but if they see that there are other needs, they are able to use their knowledge to make that assessment and to act on it. The ability to practice as a professional who came into nursing not to change ten dressings a day but to change the lives of ten people, is far greater than in the hospital sector."

In the UK, The Queen's Nursing Institute celebrated its 150-year anniversary in 2009 optimistic about the role District Nurses will play in the coming years: "The next decade of primary care expansion, which will include much more care in the patient's home supported by information and care technologies, is uniquely suited to District Nurses' specialist skills. They should have confidence that they have what primary care needs: the trust of patients and families, the unique skills to nurse in domestic settings, and the vision to lead others in this most challenging of territory."[18]

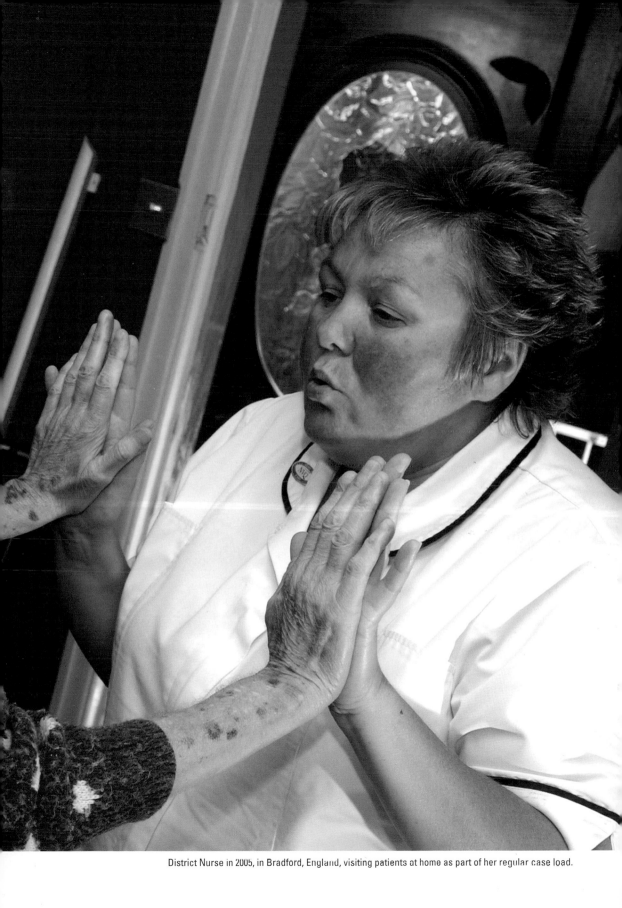

District Nurse in 2005, in Bradford, England, visiting patients at home as part of her regular case load.

Queen's Nurses leaving Buckingham Palace after the Jubilee Review with Queen Mary, June 1937. William Rathbone, a wealthy merchant and philanthropist in Liverpool, initiated the first scheme for specially trained nurses to attend to sick people in their homes. He had employed a nurse, Mary Robinson, to care for his wife at home during her final illness and, after her death, he kept Mary on for people locally who could not afford to pay for nursing, but would benefit from care in their own homes. By 1868, a District Nursing Association had been formed in East London and, in 1887, Queen Victoria devoted a large sum of money to the foundation of a training organisation—the Queen's Institute of District Nursing. The system of district nursing spread rapidly in the British Commonwealth, in European countries and throughout the world; the title "Queen's Nurse" carries a great deal of prestige. The use of the title ceased for a period in 1968, but was reintroduced in 2007, and the work continues today in the form of the Queen's Nursing Institute.[19]

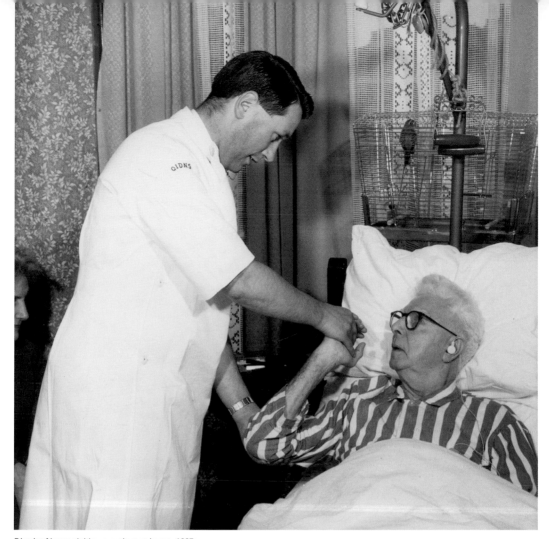

District Nurse visiting a patient at home, 1967.

The Queen's Institute of District Nursing introduced male nurses in 1947. One of those nurses, Mr DJ Gillett, wrote in the *Queen's Nurses Magazine* in 1948: "It was an experiment. There were, in Great Britain, four of us young men, setting out to prove the value and efficiency of our sex in this new sphere of nursing.

Prior to commencing duties I was naturally keenly interested and filled with conjecture as to the sort of reception I would receive, first, from the general public and, secondly, from my female counterpart. I place my female colleague second because I anticipated, and expected, a cordial welcome from her, in view of her familiarity and acceptance of the male nurse in general hospitals, fever nursing and mental nursing. With certain exceptions the old prejudice against males as nurses has disappeared from the nursing profession.

... but without exception I have been accepted gratefully and unreservedly into every home where I have had occasion to carry out nursing duties. The male nurse covers more ground at present than the Queen's Sisters, because he is only permitted to nurse male patients. This means, that to employ him fully, he nurses nearly all the male patients within the orbit of the Nursing Home; whereas, the Queen's Sister, in the cities, covers particular areas. My average daily travelling distance is 21 miles."[20]

Beyond Four Walls

Geoff Hunt's career as a District Nurse in the UK spanned 40 years. He was born in Essex in 1928, and began his nurse training at West Middlesex Hospital, near London, qualifying in 1952. We talked to him about what it means to be a Queen's Nurse.

"For a year I worked in the field of engineering. I left to join the Royal Navy as a Sick Berth Attendant (SBA) and spent three years mostly in sea-going postings as the SBA in sole charge in small ships. That was enjoyable and, when I left the Navy, I could not settle back in the factory; I decided I would follow the medical life, and became a student nurse in 1949.

As a nurse, I worked only in England but, as an SBA, I worked in Sri Lanka, Malaya, and other places where my ships called. When things were tough here in the late 50s early 60s—young, married with kids, on a very poor salary—I tried a couple of overseas postings in Indonesia and Venezuela, but both fell through because of insurrection in those countries. For those few years we were poor as church mice and I used to 'moonlight' for a while. Hard up nurses of today can have no idea how bad things were for us—mainly the male nurses—during that time."

As a District Nurse, Geoff worked in the South of England, becoming Deputy Superintendent of District Nursing in Hillingdon for four years in 1966. He was Principal Nursing Officer in Reading from 1970 and, in 1982, he became Director of Nursing Services in Wokingham until 1988, when he retired.

"I always felt that nursing was not a job enclosed within four walls and, though I never considered nursing a vocation, I did enjoy the feeling that I could spend my working days caring for and helping other people.

Nursing has changed far and away for the better. The training nurses of my generation received would probably be laughed at today, but that does not mean that we remained in the past. We had to learn about the new aspects of nursing as they came along. Any nurse has to keep abreast of changes and new methods. The change for the worse for me is the dilution of true 'bedside nursing', with an increasing dependence on the lower grades of nurses, now being called 'Care Assistants', with no real and deep knowledge behind the jobs they have to do. These exist and are becoming more popular in many countries.

Degree courses are fine, but they should contain more than the small amount of practical nursing and 'hands-on' patient care that they do at present. Perhaps nurses should have a 'pre-clinical' year as do doctors, working with other trained and experienced nurses who would impart the hidden skills that cannot be taught in the Schools of Nursing.

I am sure that nurses graduating in 2020 will have to confront attempts on their clinical freedom, such as it is. My own experience as a Nurse Manager shows me that the lay side of NHS Management has, for the last 40 years, been trying to get control of what nurses can and cannot do, mostly in attempts to reduce spending.

The need for more nurse-led research into basic patient care is vitally important. When I was a young Queen's Nurse, I was involved as a participant in Lisbeth Hockey's book, *Feeling the Pulse*, and I was involved with a 'time and motion' study as a student nurse.[21] We gave the researchers a pretty rough time at first, but explanations and their publication of the findings changed our views. Later I did some simple, and some complicated, research that was published. Nurses should get their work in print so that others can learn."

Queen's Nurse, Geoff Hunt, setting out from home in Spring 1953, in his 1938 Morris 8.

Virtual Home Visits

Telenursing is the next frontier in the nursing workplace. It involves delivering healthcare services across distances using telecommunication and information technologies. It can be as simple as a telephone call, or involve sophisticated interactive systems that transmit voice, images and data from one physical location to another. Across the globe, an explosion of telenursing programmes is underway and nurses are adapting quickly to the virtual workplace.

Not that telenursing is entirely new: the telephone has long provided a lifeline to nurses working in remote areas. But the ability to transmit ever more physiologic data remotely is now spurring the expansion of telenursing into post-hospitalization follow-up, home care and disease management. Motivating recent developments is the prospect of reducing geographic inequalities in access to care, shortening the length of hospital stays, and supporting self-management of chronic diseases. For example, in a telenursing diabetes management programme in the UK, patients apply a skin patch to measure sugars and transmit the information over the telephone. A nurse monitors these readings and calls the patient if sugars reach dangerous levels. Some believe smart toilets and t-shirts with sensors are coming soon.

Telenursing is likely to change the face of home care in many countries. Family care-givers can take on more active roles and obtain the regular support they need to do so. The International Council of Nurses (ICN) reports that 46 per cent of home nursing visits in America could be replaced by telenursing, cutting costs by half and expanding demand for telenurses significantly.

Nurses are playing a vital role not just in providing telenursing services but also in developing systems that allow them to provide high quality patient care from a distance. Krisan Palmer, a cardiac nurse in New Brunswick, Canada, began developing telenursing systems after an allergy to latex put her in anaphylactic shock. No longer able to treat patients at the Heart Centre in person, she became involved in designing remote patient monitoring systems. Now Telehealth Coordinator for one of the Regional Health Authorities in New Brunswick, Palmer was named Wired Woman of the Year by the International Wired Women's Society in 2009 and is recognised in Canada and internationally as a major health systems innovator.

Palmer's first venture into telenursing, in 1998, was a programme designed to follow Heart Centre patients at home after they underwent revascularisation procedures. The Centre serves a large, mostly rural population and patients would normally remain in hospital for five days and be discharged home with instructions to follow up with their family doctors and return to the Heart Centre six to eight weeks later. However, a study undertaken by one of the surgeons found that a third of these patients visited their local ER within nine days of discharge, many with wound infections, atrial fibrillation or heart failure. The Centre's director proposed a visionary way to deal with follow-up care for these patients: virtual nurse visits at home.

Nurses were initially very uncomfortable with the technology, but as soon as they had a patient in front of them, the technology disappeared and the relationship took over. The video component is essential to that and is something Palmer fought hard to keep in the system design. The ability to touch patients had been taken away; seeing them was essential. Some nurses worried they would miss getting to know patients and their families, but this concern soon evaporated as they met grandchildren, dogs and neighbours during tele-monitoring visits. The technology actually promoted holistic care.

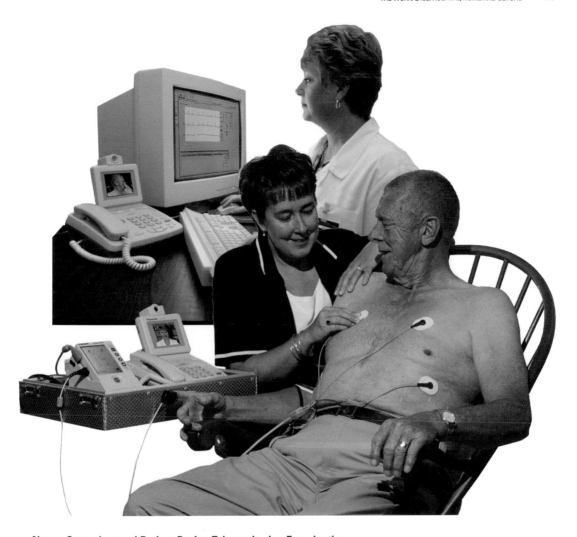

Nurse, Care-giver and Patient During Telemonitoring Examination

+ Following his revascularisation surgery, the patient brings the equipment home upon discharge and plugs it into a normal telephone outlet. He is given a daily appointment schedule with the follow-up nurse.

+ Prior to the call, the patient (or care-giver) weighs himself and takes his temperature to provide the nurse with this information. He then sits in front of the unit and attaches the blood pressure cuff, the four electrocardiogram leads and a finger clip to monitor oxygen saturation. He wears something that makes it easy for the nurse to examine the wound incision and graft harvest site through the video camera.

+ When the nurse calls, the push of a button transmits the vital signs data to the central station. Then the nurse connects via videophone to complete the clinical assessment.

+ The nurse is able to consult with various medical specialists on clinical presentations that are cause for concern and these can be detected and treated before they become urgent. The most common problems are atrial fibrillation, wound infection and fluid retention.

Lois Scott in her office at the Moncton Call Centre, 2002.

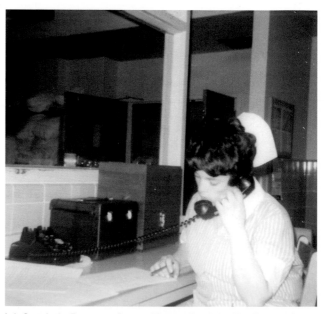

Lois Scott in the Emergency Room at Moncton Hospital in New Brunswick, Canada, 1971.

Filling the Gaps in Care

Lois Scott, RN, MScN, is founding member of the Telenursing Advisory Group of the International Society of Telemedicine and E-health, and of the International Council of Nurses TeleNursing Network. In these roles, she is helping to guide the global development of tele-nursing. As Vice-President of Care-Enhanced Solutions at McKesson Canada, she is looking at ways to expand the applications of telenursing into chronic disease management. We talked to her about the challenge of getting new programmes up and running.

Lois Scott is an internationally-recognised pioneer in telenursing whose career has brought her from the Emergency Department (ED) at The Moncton Hospital in New Brunswick, Canada, to the Department of Health of a provincial government and most recently into the private sector, where she has led the business and clinical development of a broad range of telehealth programmes.

In all of these activities, her primary focus remains the clinical care of patients. "I believe the essence of nursing is caring and helping people cope with health-related situations. One of my most meaningful nursing moments happened many years ago, when I was holding a young boy's hand as casts were being put on his legs. He was understandably anxious; however, when the procedure was finished, he quietly said "Your hands feel just like my Mommy's." I considered this one of the biggest compliments that I could ever receive from any child. It also taught me that it is not the remarkable things that nurses do that make the most difference, but the simple things that help people cope."

After receiving a diploma in nursing from The Moncton Hospital School of Nursing, Scott found her fit in the ED, thriving on the chaos and variety of people who came through the doors. It was there that she started building systems to improve care. The first was an ED triage system; then a poison control programme that sought to prevent incidents as well as treat current crises. In this position, she networked with public health nurses, psychologists, mental health clinics and school social workers. Scott recognised the challenge of finding moments for teaching when people would be most receptive to the message.

"I was always looking at gaps", says Scott, "and I loved designing programmes to fill them." Scott credits working in a progressive and supportive environment as paving the way to innovation in healthcare. The Moncton Hospital was supportive of its nurses' efforts to pioneer new ideas. Director of Nursing Katherine Wright and hospital CEO, Bill Kilpatrick, encouraged their talented nurses to share the ideas they developed, speak at conferences and contribute to national programmes. And there was money to support these activities. Several years earlier, Kilpatrick asked the Moncton Hospital School of Nursing Alumni to operate the hospital's coffee shop. Some of the profits from this business were used to provide funds for Alumni members to pursue post-diploma education, including tuition, books and travel expenses and to attend nursing-related conferences. Scott completed her Bachelors and Masters Degrees in Nursing on a part-time basis with the support of funding from the Alumni. She also participated on a large number of provincial and national committees, such as starting an ED Manager's Network for New Brunswick, co-chairing a federal initiative on workforce management for EDs, and working with professional and industry associations on issues like professional standards and certification exams.

From Stethoscope to Telephone

Scott's Masters' thesis asked the question "What prompts non-urgent patients to seek emergency care?" Her conclusion was that non-urgent patients had high levels of uncertainty that caused them to be anxious; EDs were often viewed as the way to cope. She thought there might be a way to build a telehealth service on the the poison control model, which would allow patients with non-urgent symptoms to access information and allay anxiety via telephone and prevent unnecessary ED visits.

Scott submitted a Telecare proposal to New Brunswick's Department of Health, but it was not approved. At that point, she realised it might be easier to promote the programme and influence decisions from inside the system. "If you can influence policy and budgets then that's where it's happening and where you have to be", she thought.

Three years at the Department of Health taught her the internal workings of government, policymaking, programme development, evaluation and public accountability. "It satisfied my building impulse", she states.

She was able to sell the idea of teletriage within the Department of Health and a pilot project in the Moncton area was approved in 1996, with Scott as the government representative on the implementation committee.

At first the nurses were employed by Moncton's two hospitals and worked from designated offices within the EDs; however, this did not work out very well, as the needs of the EDs often took priority over those of the Telecare Service. If the EDs were short-staffed, Telecare nurses were sometimes reassigned, either leaving the Telecare service under resourced or totally suspended. "In the meantime", Scott recalls, "people were calling and could not get through, which undermined the public's trust in the service being readily available 24/7." This and other problems led the Advisory Committee to question whether the service should be based inside or out of hospitals.

At this time, New Brunswick's government under the leadership of Premier Frank McKenna was promoting use of the information highway, enhanced and equitable access to healthcare for all residents and an aggressive Economic Development strategy, including private-public partnerships. An Economic Development representative met with a member of a Montréal-based company that was developing a software solution for physician offices. After reviewing New Brunswick's Telecare service, the company decided to negotiate a public-private partnership with the government of New Brunswick. They also approached Scott to see if she would be interested in directing the programme for them.

Scott decided to make the move to the private sector. "We started in New Brunswick and saw the establishment of the country's first publicly-funded province-wide triage and health information line provided by a private sector company." With the help of a very committed and competent team, Scott implemented similar services for Ontario, the Northwest Territories, Newfoundland and Labrador and the federal Department of National Defense. The clinical guidelines and programme infrastructure first tested in New Brunswick were also used for the other provinces. "Canadians are often cynical of private sector involvement in the delivery of healthcare", says Scott, "but in reality 40 per cent of healthcare services in Canada are, and have been, provided by private sector organisations. And private sector employees have the same passion and commitment to safety quality, efficiency and effectiveness as is seen in the public sector." She also found it easier to get things done quickly in the private sector. It was less bulky, and the business contract with clearly stated outcomes proved a valuable means of guaranteeing that things get done in the expected way. She also found the level of accountability for individual nurses, for the team and for the company to be much clearer and more directive. And there were rewards for risk and success which differed from the the public sector where it is not always easy to acknowledge and reward high achievers.

Human Resources in Telenursing

"My bias going into teletriage was that ED nurses would be best suited", Scott admits. But that concept did not stand the test of time. She learned that the art of teletriage was really to assess symptoms and determine where and when a person should go for the most appropriate care. "Some nurses are really good at developing a therapeutic relationship very quickly, which leads to the patient trusting them and following their advice", says Scott. She found that the skills needed to provide quality telenursing services do not belong to any one set of nurses. The competencies of an ideal teletriage nurse include clinical and communication skills, multitasking—the ability to type, listen, process and read at the same time—strong clinical decision making capacity and critical thinking. "It took us a while to identify those competencies, but we now look for them when we interview candidates", says Scott. Across Canada, most of the nurses recruited as telenurses have many years of experience.

In 2007, Scott assumed the position of Vice-President of Care-Enhanced Solutions at McKesson Canada. McKesson is a large multi-national corporation that has, for the last 12 years, provided telehealth services for millions of Americans, including chronic disease management services for Medicare and Medicaid populations in several US states, as well as teletriage, mental health and disease management programmes for the population of Australia and New Zealand. Scott considers chronic disease management the next significant extension to telehealth services and is now considering how the tools McKesson has developed in other countries can work best within the Canadian context.

"McKesson has excellent tools", Scott has found, "to coach patients to self-manage their chronic conditions, help predict when people with certain chronic diseases are apt to be require hospitalisation and help patients adhere to medication therapies."

Some nurses are really good at developing a therapeutic relationship very quickly, which leads to the patient trusting them and following their advice.

During the last year, Scott led the planning and implementation of a telecare programme for the province of Nova Scotia, which includes symptom management, health information and a community information service. Nova Scotia's Department of Health has stated its interest in building more services into their core Telecare programme as funding becomes available. Chronic Disease Management and Wellness Coaching are on their list.

Care Moves Into the Living Room

Healthcare has shifted dramatically in the past few decades, from acute care in institutions to ambulatory clinics, to community based care. Telenursing enables caregivers to take one step further and allow people to access care from their living rooms, workplaces or schools on a 24/7 basis. Telehealth services also enable more efficient use of health professionals. Labour-intensive activities like teaching and self care coaching can be provided remotely by telenurses, with face-to-face encounters reserved for more complex care. Telehealth also allows nurses who cannot handle the physical demands of hospital-based nursing to remain actively employed in their profession. Considering that the current shortage of nurses is predicted to increase dramatically in the next decade, any way to keep nurses working longer is worthwhile.

Increasingly, telenurses are working not in agencies or offices, but from home, receiving orientation and continuing education by distance. In the US, there are approximately 1,000 McKesson nurses working from home. In Nova Scotia, 44 nurses are working from their homes in every region of the province and are being supervised in "real time" by Clinical Team Leaders in Halifax.

Going Global

As the development of telenursing picks up speed in many countries, the need for international collaboration has become apparent. In 2008, Scott, along with Dr Loretta Schlachta Fairchild and Diane Castelli, of the US, worked with the International Society of Telemedicine and E-health to form a Telenursing Advisory Group. Scott hosted the first international meeting of this group in Ottawa in 2009. In addition, Scott and her colleagues believed that affiliation with the International Council of Nurses (ICN) would allow them to reach a broader population of nurses throughout the world and focus on issues specific to nurses. They held the inaugural meeting of the ICN TeleNursing Network in Durban, South Africa, later in 2009. ICN convened an advisory committee with representatives from seven regions, each of whom has played a leadership role in telenursing in their part of the world. As Canada's representative, Scott noted: "There is a lot of experience and wisdom to share and we can use this to support countries and organizations that are starting programmes." There is growing interest in telehealth in the developing world, especially as cell phone coverage expands. This has been focused primarily on support for health workers in remote areas, but is quickly expanding to provide telehealth services to general populations.

Scott's focus today is to develop, both in Canada and internationally, accreditation standards for telenursing programmes to ensure that these services, whether public or private, are of the highest quality and that telenurses are equipped with the education, monitoring and support they need to work in this evolving area of nursing practice.

Beyond the Comfort Zone

Lieutenant Amy Zayek, severe trauma nurse with the Female Corpsman Team, holds an Afghan child during a patrol, Afghanistan, 2010.

Carol Etherington with a group of physicians in Kosovo. They had never been trained in psychological trauma, but were willing to learn in order to help their patients.

Human Rights Begin at Home

Carol Etherington, RN, MScN, from Nashville, Tennessee, has designed and implemented community-based programmes for people living in the aftermath of war and natural disaster in Bosnia, Poland, Honduras, Tajikistan, Kosovo, Sierra Leone and Angola. She has worked throughout the US during times of natural and man made disasters including earthquakes, hurricanes, school shootings, and New York City post 9/11. She was awarded the International Achievement Award by the International Council of Nurses' Florence Nightingale International Foundation (FNIF) in 2003. She took a moment to contribute her thoughts on nurses' work in upholding human rights, at home and abroad.

Carol Etherington is an Associate Director of Vanderbilt's Institute for Global Health and teaches medical, nursing and interdisciplinary groups of graduate students in community health, global health, and caring for victims of violence. Etherington is an outspoken advocate for underserved and vulnerable populations and strongly promotes the concept that health, mental health, human rights and human dignity are inextricably linked.

"Growing up, I did not believe I wanted to be a nurse, a teacher or in the service professions— the first several years in college I majored in journalism with a minor in political science. That did not, however, give me what I wanted and, after working a semester at a medical center in Central Kentucky, I knew that I wanted a career that would allow me to interact with people in a very unique and special way. Nursing absolutely fit that criteria

and after, almost 40 years of experiencing it in every conceivable setting and situation, I can say that it has more than lived up to being THE profession which has allowed me to do most everything I have ever wanted. If I had seven lifetimes, at least six of them would be as a nurse.

I began my career in Appalachia, a place of great beauty and resilient people, a place possessed of extraordinary natural resources and environmental riches. It had taken less than a century for the land and the people to be exploited, manipulated and ravaged. Less than a century for the population to be left with staggering percentages of chronic illness, intense hopelessness, pervasive feelings of helplessness and a lot of corrupt and greedy people in power. In the later stages of my career, as I became more and more involved in international health, I found so many of the same dynamics to be true. There are striking parallels whenever and wherever there are combinations of environmental riches, corruption and greed, and there is resulting chaos and mayhem for populations who happen to be living in the wrong place at the wrong time in history.

I spent almost 20 years working in a metropolitan police department and, in those early years of my career, I saw a health system often negligent, ineffective and value laden in its response to victims of violence. I saw a legal system inefficient and ineffective, at times dismissive of the seriousness of violence—often until a tragedy of such magnitude occurred that it could not be ignored. The response, or lack of, seemed particularly true for victims of sexual assault or intra family violence. While many countries have made major strides within their health and criminal justice systems these past decades, I am struck by the parallels of what is occurring to victims on a global level. Rape is used as a strategy of war, children of seven or eight are conscripted, brainwashed and empowered with a weapon that they can barely carry, an estimated two million women and children are sold or brokered into the bondage of sweat shops or brothels. As I became more aware of the striking parallels from those early years and what I saw with individual victims, with what is happening to whole populations around the globe, I came to realise that, whether at home or abroad, health is inextricably linked to human rights. That is the health and human rights of an individual, a family, a race, an ethnic group or a nation. While many people believe that they meld health and human rights in their everyday practice, there are far, far too few who are specifically, intentionally and loudly proclaiming attention to it at national and international levels.

Since those early years, I have worked in humanitarian crises in Cambodia, Bosnia, Poland, Kosovo, Honduras, Tajikistan, Sierra Leone, Angola, Eastern Chad and the US; in a non-crisis capacity in Kenya, Mozambique, China and Guatemala.

One of the most basic challenges of working in various countries has, for me, been trying to learn at least a modicum of words and phrases in each one. There is the added responsibility of not only assessing the current situation but understanding the history and the infrastructure that existed before the catastrophic event—and in the case of war, repetitive events.

When war comes to a country, infrastructures collapse. The healthcare system, often already fragile, collapses along with the education system, the economy, and the labour system. All the entities that keep the fabric of daily life running are gone. Communities that do not feel the direct impact of bombs are overrun by people fleeing the communities that do. There is a clash of cultures, creating tensions and resentment within, even though they might be aligned by religion or politics or simply their shared hatred of the oppressor. Schools close and are inhabited by the displaced; workplaces close and, in cold climates, even in the midst of a hot summer, families will be seen selling their belongings to ensure there is heat for the winter. The elderly become a burden—and feel that way. They are often the ones who, by choice or necessity, are left when others flee.

As war continues there is adaptation. The drudgery of seeking out food, clean water and shelter becomes a daily way of life and obtaining those things takes every ounce of energy. There is not much left over for nurturing and protecting children. With energy needed for sheer physical endurance, there is nothing left to cope with emotional wounds except "numbing" which is an effective tool for emotional survival.

There are no global truths about how people experience war or respond to trauma. Today, more research than ever before is being done on the medical, psychological and social response to complex emergencies. Thankfully, nurses, are involved in many of these efforts, though too infrequently, are we at the table asking the tough questions and making people uncomfortable. We need to be much more active and visceral in our questioning.

In this age when so many nurses want to work in a global setting that is at least an ocean away from their daily life, it is important to remember that global health includes our own backyards. Eleanor Roosevelt once said that "human rights begin at home". Vulnerable populations are everywhere and, whether you are working with malnourished in Appalachia or Angola, whether children are orphaned by AIDS in Harlem or Malawi, there is a need for awareness, and for nurses to be courageous, passionate and wise in acting and speaking out on behalf of their populations.

Carol Etherington with a young child in the Darfur camps of eastern Chad.

Wartime Nursing

When we lie ill at home surrounded with comfort, we never think of feeling any special gratitude for the sick-room delicacies which we accept as a consequence of our illness; but the poor officer lying ill and weary in his crazy hut, dependent for the merest necessaries of existence upon a clumsy, ignorant soldier-cook, who would almost prefer eating his meat raw to having the trouble of cooking it (our English soldiers are bad campaigners), often finds his greatest troubles in the want of those little delicacies with which a weak stomach must be humoured into retaining nourishment.... Don't you think, reader, if you were lying, with parched lips and fading appetite, thousands of miles from mother, wife, or sister, loathing the rough food by your side, and thinking regretfully of that English home where nothing that could minister to your great need would be left untried—don't you think that you would welcome the familiar figure of the stout lady whose bony horse has just pulled up at the door of your hut, and whose panniers contain some cooling drink, a little broth, some homely cake, or a dish of jelly or blanc-mange....

Mary Seacole, *Wonderful Adventures of Mrs Seacole in Many Lands*, 1857.

Mary Seacole (1805–1881) was a nurse probably best known for her part in the Crimean War. One of Seacole's key beliefs was in the importance of a soldier's diet, outlined in her autobiography *Wonderful Adventures of Mary Seacole in Many Lands*, published in 1857.
OPPOSITE *Nurses & Midwifes are needed. The war time job that can be your career*, Second World War poster.

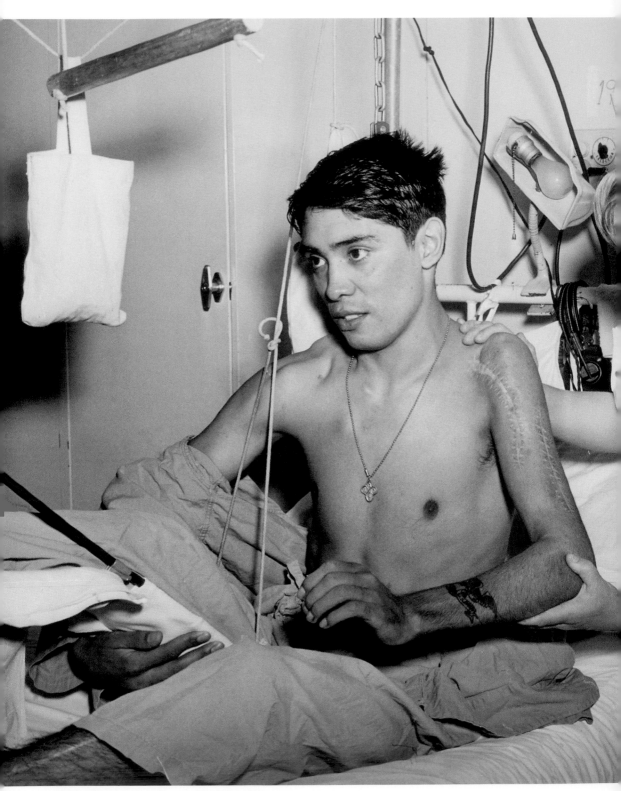

A nurse helps an American Second World War soldier.

"We're nurses, we all know we have most urgent business ahead of us. We nurses are the only women who go right up front with the soldiers. If we weren't serious, we wouldn't have taken the Army oath, or the Florence Nightingale Pledge, in the first place. I don't have to remind you", Cherry said with some difficulty, and her voice dropped, "that we are here to dedicate our lives so that others may live."

Cherry Ames, in *Chief Nurse*, 1944.

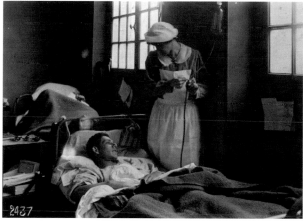

A Red Cross nurse attends a soldier at US American National Red Cross Hospital No 1, Paris, France, during the First World War.

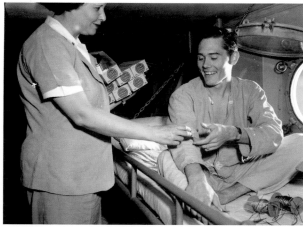

A nurse gives out packets of Lucky Strike cigarettes to wounded soldiers on the Second World War hospital ship, Algonquin.

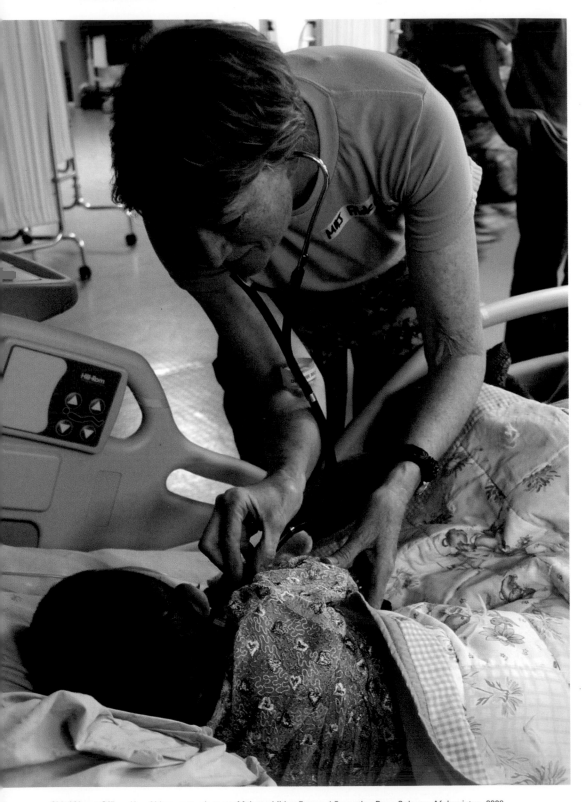

Chief Nurse Officer Una Alderman tends to an Afghan child at Forward Operating Base Salerno, Afghanistan, 2009.

Dr Peter Carter, General Secretary of the Royal College of Nursing, with nurses in Afghanistan, 2009.

I will never forget the inspirational care and courage of our nursing staff in Afghanistan, Basra and at the Royal Centre for Defence Medicine at Selly Oak in Birmingham.

Having visited Iraq and Afghanistan, I was struck by the incredible work of nursing staff in such challenging situations. These nurses are among the unsung heroes of our efforts overseas, offering advanced care and pushing back the boundaries of modern day nursing in a setting that is worlds apart from life in the UK. The bravery of these nurses, both regulars and reservists, exists alongside the high level of skill required to treat complex problems in a very difficult environment.

Dr Peter Carter, General Secretary, Royal College of Nursing.

Christiane Roth, a nurse from Switzerland, with women from Matame, Zinder Province, Niger. Niger represents one of the largest malnutrition-treatment programmes in MSF's history, with a capacity for treating 20,000 severely malnourished children per year, through five therapeutic feeding centres and 27 ambulatory centres.

Ghislaine Télémaque was the nurse aboard the research ship Amundsen in 2008. Here, she accompanies the crew during an expedition onto the ice cap.

Ghislaine Télémaque at the clinic in Nemaska, 2010.

Forgotten Corners of the World

Ghislaine Télémaque, RN, was born in Haiti and moved to Québec with her family in 1970. She studied nursing and spent eight years working in hospital Emergency Rooms and intensive care units in Montréal. In 1986, she signed on with Oxfam and has since divided her time between clinic nursing in the far north of Québec and relief work with international agencies. She described some of the features of nursing in these different contexts that make the hardships worthwhile.

"My mission with Oxfam was to create primary care services in the Dominican Republic's vast sugar plantations, called bateys, where thousands of migrant Haitian labourers worked. Many started with seasonal contracts but ended up staying on, status-less, with no access to health services or education for their children. The situation received significant media attention, with conditions described as neo-slavery. I followed the situation in the bateys through human rights groups in Montréal, and was driven by a desire to help people from the country where I was born."

In the two years she spent in the Dominican Republic, Télémaque opened primary care centres in a number of bateys, working with local Non-Governmental Organisations (NGOs) to provide services to workers and their families. They established vaccination, prenatal care and health promotion programmes, and set up a kindergarten. The centre was located within the batey itself, where workers could easily come to receive care. When Télémaque's contract finished in 1988, the local NGO continued to run the centre.

Nursing opens doors to getting involved in protecting human rights. We serve as witnesses to what's happening, and do some small things to help.

She crossed the island into Haiti to see if there were a way to establish herself in the country following the fall of the dictator Baby Doc Duvalier. It was time of great optimism but also chaos in the country. Télémaque worked with UNICEF and a number of other international NGOs and even assumed the position of Directrice nationale des Soins infirmiers within the Ministry of Health for a brief six months before the coup d'état against President Aristide in 1991. When things refused to settle down in the months following the coup, Télémaque decided it was time to return to Montréal.

But a return to hospital nursing was not on the agenda. After a short while in Local Community Health Centres (CLSCs in Québec) she responded to an ad recruiting nurses to work in the far north of Québec for the Cree Health Board.

Northern Nursing

Since 1992, she has worked in villages all over the North. Each has a clinic that provides community health programmes and chronic disease management. While the clinics are similar in many ways to CLSCs, nurses work much more independently. A CLSC nurse in the "South" will triage patients before a doctor examines them. In the North, nurses assess the patient, conduct a general exam and arrive at a diagnosis. They reassure the patient and provide a treatment, and if medication is needed, they dispense it, as there is no pharmacy business in the village. The only pharmacy is actually inside the clinic and is managed by nurses.

"We have an extended scope of practice and are allowed to do things we can't do down south", says Télémaque. She emphasises that they are also trained to do them, receiving special certification for each new skill set.

A typical day in the Nemaska health centre where she has worked since Autumn 2009 starts with a walk-in clinic and thankfully there are not the hours-long waits experienced elsewhere in Québec. "People expect to be seen right away up here", says Télémaque. She sees the whole gamut of health complaints and most often handles them on her own. A doctor comes to Nemaska for about one week a month, and sees chronic patients Télémaque and the other nurses have referred for follow-up.

Medical evacuations are used for more urgent cases. The planes arrive from Rouyn Noranda or Val d'Or and transport patients to the appropriate referral hospital. There is a regional hospital in Chiassibi, north of Radisson. Patients in need of surgery must travel to Val d'Or, or Rouyn Noranda or Amos. Small planes, mostly Cesnas, are the primary means of transport between villages and larger centres. All pregnant women are flown out of the village at 36 weeks gestation to spend the last part of their pregnancy close to a hospital. When labour starts before 35 weeks, the nurses may end up delivering the baby.

The load can be overwhelming. "There are times, when I was alone on call and needed to go out two or three times each night, I think about leaving and not coming back", Télémaque admits. "But so far I always have." The community appreciates those who return year after year. "We're familiar faces, and that's reassuring to people here. They appreciate that." But there are limits to how involved the nurses become. "It's their community and we're not there to change it", says Télémaque.

Nemaska is a village of 650 people. It has one grocery store. The only real industry is Air Creebec. Other jobs are mainly in local government and services, but unemployment is high. The village is pretty, sitting on the shores of lake Champion, far enough south that there are still a few small evergreens. The cold does not bother Télémaque. "I prefer winter here over Montréal. It may be cold, but at least it's dry and doesn't get into your bones", she says. "I make a point of walking around the village every morning, no matter what temperature. I dress well and take a ski pole because there are a lot of dogs and they like to follow me."

Télémaque shares duty with three other nurses. She keeps an apartment in Montréal for the limited time she spends there and generally lives in shared housing available to workers in the various northern villages. However, she decided recently to take on a regular position in Nemaska and now has her own house there.

During the summer she often works on the ice breakers run by the Department of Fisheries and Oceans, which are required by law to have a health professional on board when the vessels travel in Arctic area. She heads out to sea with a crew of up to 78–100 people and spends six weeks on the round trip to the Arctic.

Humanitarian Missions

The flexibility of northern nursing is attractive as it enables Télémaque to devote part of each year to humanitarian missions around the globe. She had hesitated to accept a mission this year because of the post-earthquake turmoil in Haiti, but was not in a rush to be among the first arrivals. "There will always be a need in Haiti. I'm not in a big hurry."

Télémaque started going on missions with Médecins Sans Frontières (Doctors Without Borders) in the 2000s, but has worked in the past with various NGOs (Médecins du Monde, Oxfam, Enfants du Monde) in Chad, Afghanistan immediately after the Gulf War in 2003 and most recently Congo. "They call me to propose a mission and I tell them whether I'm available", she explains. "The kind of mission I accept is one where I can be useful and put my skills and organisational abilities to work and help train local nurses. It's very gratifying." Living conditions are very basic, but that's not a problem for her. "In Montréal I live well", she says, "but when I go abroad I'm ready for anything. Conditions are often very difficult, but I tell myself it's not forever."

Malnutrition and violence against women and girls are what haunts her the most about the places she works overseas. "It is hard to see children in that condition", she admits. "And to see the social situations that bring people to a condition of malnutrition."

Télémaque will stay in a country for six or seven months. These are complicated countries, chaotic and often dangerous. "We take precautions and respect security measures", she states. "You always have to be on guard and be prudent, but you can't let fear take over."

She rarely works with the same people twice. A group of doctors and nurses will come together for six months and then disband. "People go on missions for different reasons", she finds. Some do it once as a way to fulfill a dream or ambition, and do not return. For Télémaque it is her form of social engagement: to go places others will not, to witness, and to do some small things to help.

A Modern Day Black Bag

Whether she is packing to return up north or leaving on an overseas mission, Télémaque's bag is sure to include two essential items: her palm pilot and her stethoscope. She keeps the palm pilot updated with vital reference works and guidelines and brings it along wherever she is working. She also invested in a good quality stethoscope and guards it carefully. "There are stethoscopes in the clinics up north, but I hear better with mine. When I listen to someone's lungs, I want to hear well. We do not have X-Rays in the clinic up north or on the field." A small hard drive loaded with music and medical references go into the bag as well, and once again, Télémaque is ready for departure.

A child being weighed at a feeding centre in Chad, 2007.

Mothers patiently wait their turn at the mobile clinic, Chad, 2007.

4
Transforming Care

Transforming Care

Nurses today are facing new care environments that reflect changing population needs and a dramatic expansion in healthcare technologies and know-how. Expectations are high and resources, especially healthcare providers, are limited. In this Chapter, we look at how care is being transformed to cope with these demands and what role nurses are playing in the transformation.

Team practice is being emphasised as a way to make best use of each of the professionals involved in care. We begin with a look at the long but choppy history of interprofessional practice in the US that is energised today by the patient safety agenda. Fostering mutual respect between doctors and nurses is a vital part of this work. A retired head nurse recalls the features of her Neonatal Intensive Care Unit (NICU) that enhanced teamwork, and a counterpart in Brazil describes how parents are now included as part of the team caring for these tiny infants. Yumi Tamura, a pioneer in Interprofessional Education in Japan, recounts how the relief effort mounted following the 1995 earthquake in Kobe brought nurses, doctors, other health professionals and volunteers into highly constructive teams, and describes what has been done to perpetuate collaboration beyond the relief setting.

Maureen Shawn Kennedy, Interim Editor-in-Chief of *The American Journal of Nursing*, expresses dismay at the lack of influence nurses are perceived to have on healthcare policy, despite general agreement that this should be otherwise. She traces nurses' long history as architects of change to emphasise the role they should be playing at this defining moment in American healthcare.

The UK is currently undertaking a vast campaign called "Dignity: At the Heart of Everything We Do" which brings to the fore many of the tenets espoused by Florence Nightingale herself. The elements of dignified care—compassion, sensitivity, privacy and respect—are too often sacrificed in today's care environment. It has become clear in the campaign that the ability to provide dignified care is contingent on the dignity accorded to the nursing profession.

PREVIOUS PAGES Students relax in the nurses' residence, Washington University School of Nursing, 1944. The nurse standing is wearing the uniform of the US Cadet Nurse Corps, a programme established by the federal government to meet the wartime nursing shortage. OPPOSITE Community nurse, Essex, England, 2007.

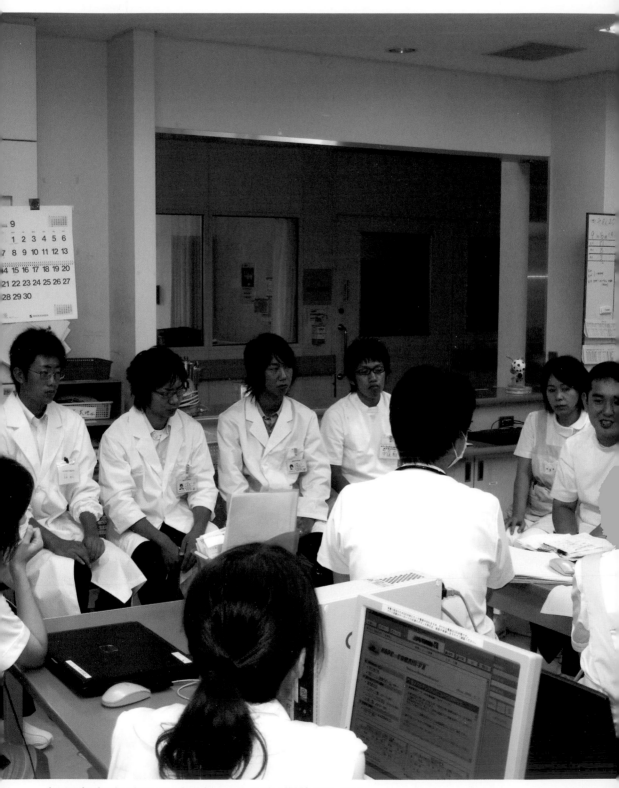

Interprofessional student group observing a team meeting, KIPEC, Kobe, Japan.

Team-based Practice

Interprofessional practice involves two or more health professionals bringing their unique skills and knowledge together to assist patients. It has a long and complex history, as it touches everything from education to professional definition, standing and scope of practice. In the United States (US), team-based care became entrenched early on in areas such as rehabilitation, mental health, geriatric care and palliative medicine, while progress in other areas, especially primary care, has been more difficult.

Today, efforts to improve patient safety have galvanised interest in interprofessional collaboration. The Institute of Medicine has called for the "integration of observations, eyes and expertise from various health professions..." in order to optimise care.[1]

History of Interprofessional Practice in the United States

DeWitt C Baldwin, Professor Emeritus of Psychiatry and Behavioral Sciences at the University of Nevada, is one of the principal historians of interdisciplinary care teams in the US. He traces their development back to the Second World War, where teams of doctors and nurses were used extensively and successfully in the field. After the war, President Johnson's Great Society included a vision of interprofessional teams working in community care clinics to make health services more broadly available to the population.[2]

One of the first examples of interdisciplinary primary care in the US was the hospital outreach programme at the Montefiore Hospital in New York City, started in 1948 by Dr Martin Cherkasky.[3] Physicians, social workers and nurses worked in teams to provide home care to patients. During the 1960s, students of medicine and nursing supported interdisciplinary primary care projects, and many worked during the summer in community clinics based on this model. The war on poverty added momentum to the movement and Neighbourhood Health Centre Guidelines issued in 1967 emphasised the benefits of team practice.

One early example was the Martin Luther King Community Health Centre in New York City, which employed eight primary healthcare teams, each composed of an internist, pediatrician, nurse and family health worker. Each team was responsible for 3,500 patients. Kaiser Permanente, the first health maintenance organisation of importance in the US, pioneered the notion of managed care using interprofessional teams. Part of its stated aim was to keep the well 'well', not just treat the sick.[4]

Teamwork and the Safety Agenda

More recently, the patient safety agenda has re-ignited interest in team-based practice in the US. The 1999 Institute of Medicine (IOM) report "To Err is Human", found that as many as 98,000 people die in any given year from medical errors in hospitals, more than die from motor vehicle accidents, breast cancer, or AIDS. These data were extrapolated from studies conducted in Colorado, Utah and New York, which found that adverse events occurred in between 2.9 and 3.7 per cent of hospitalisations, and that between 6.6 and 13.6 per cent of adverse events led to death. Both studies found that over half of adverse events resulted from medical errors and could have been prevented. Interprofessional collaboration figured prominently among solutions for improving patient safety.[5]

In 2002 the IOM held a follow-up interdisciplinary summit that came up with a set of core competencies for the new health system that needed to be integrated into health professions education: "All health professionals should be educated to deliver patient-centred care as members of an interdisciplinary team, emphasising evidence-based practice, quality improvement approaches, and informatics."[6]

As the advantages of teamwork were stressed in these reports, it became apparent that too little was known about "what constitutes effective team performance, how it is created and nurtured, and how it directly or indirectly influences care delivery outcomes". This assumed greater importance as research on healthcare quality was finding that the majority of medical errors were caused by human factors associated with interpersonal interactions.

Healthcare is rife with status-driven hierarchical processes, the type that are known from research conducted in different industries to undermine problem-solving activities in teams. Studies in long-term healthcare settings found that the less hierarchy there was in the interaction of team members, the better were patient outcomes.

We need to find ways of working together in a context of ever-changing teams. Madeline Schmitt

The IOM follow-up report found that interdisciplinary assessment and treatment create opportunities to improve diagnosis, reduce omissions in care, and reduce avoidable error. Teams can identify areas with a high potential for error and take steps to prevent these. Examples include implementation of a recommended dilutions chart or standardised labeling of intravenous bags, tubes, and pumps.

However, breakdowns in interdisciplinary communication can result in error. Dr Madeline Schmitt, Professor Emeritus at the University of Rochester School of Nursing, reviewed malpractice suits where interactions between nurses and doctors were an issue for the IOM summit report. She found that breakdowns resulted either from doctors ignoring information communicated by nurses, or nurses failing to communicate relevant information.[7]

Their review of team practice led the IOM to recognise that "Clearly, interpersonal communication, regard for others, a strong focus on patient safety goals, and constant reassessment of the environment are important aspects of the relationship between team performance and care delivery outcomes."

Interprofessional Education

Practice is changing because of the safety agenda, but the education side has been dragging its feet. The IOM found a major disconnect between the silo approach to professional education and increasing expectations for interdisciplinary team-based care. Interprofessional Education (IPE) is meant to prepare people for collaborative practice. The question that has been difficult to answer, and that has cast a cloud of doubt over any number of efforts, is whether teaching people together will enable them to practice together better.

Nurses in Africa during the Second World War.

Dr Schmitt has developed interprofessional care models, studied their impact and developed training programmes to improve collaboration between health professions for over 40 years in the US and internationally. In a talk she gave in November 2009 at the University of Virginia, Dr Schmitt stated: "We have learned that teams are one way to delivery care together, but not the only way. Teamwork is something else: it involves learning to work together, cooperate, coordinate the timing, sequence and accuracy of actions, and collaborate on difficult problems using collective wisdom to gain insight into problems we could not solve otherwise."[8]

Dr Schmitt traced the stop and start efforts at promoting IPE in the US. As far back as 1972, the IOM held a conference on Education for the Health Team, which supported the need for interdisciplinary education to prepare medical and nursing students for collaborative work. The Institute for Health Team Development was started with funding from the Robert Wood Johnson Foundation in 1971, enabling a number of training programmes to get off the ground. In the mid-1970s, the federal Bureau of Manpower's Office of Interdisciplinary Programs funded a number of universities and medical centres to train students. However, most government and other educational funding dried up after 1980. IPE was often regarded as an expensive luxury that had no measurable impact on patient outcomes.

New programmes are now emerging at a number of universities that emphasise experiential, problem-based and situational learning. Dr Schmitt pointed to one at the University of British Columbia in Canada where health professionals tour high schools together to talk about their own health professions. This serves not only the primary purpose of generating interest among the next generation, but also allows professionals to find out more about each other. In another training programme, medical residents take on the role of a nurse, and conduct activities alongside him or her. The experience proved so powerful it is now a programme requirement.

Dr Schmitt concluded:

Our professional identity has developed in those silos. The challenge now is to discover that our self, our identity, has an interprofessional piece.

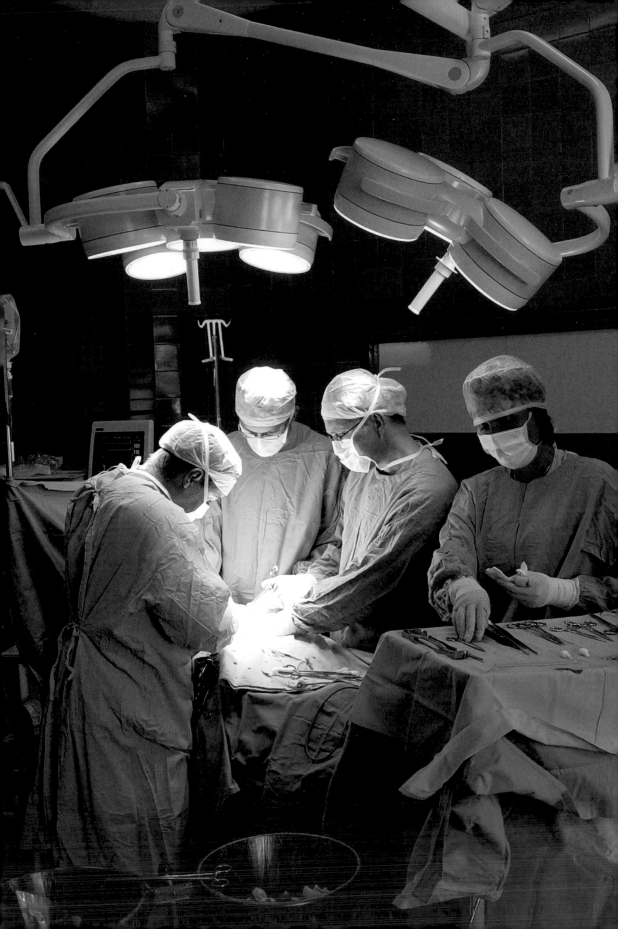

Nurse-Doctor Relations

In his article "Territoriality and power in the health professions", DeWitt Baldwin sees four ways in which nurses can claim a portion of the territory traditionally held by physicians:

+ By co-opting or taking over medical tasks and functions by force or subterfuge.

+ By seeking to gain the support of powerful allies such as the law, the courts and public opinion.

+ By seeking out newly-defined or abandoned territories.

+ By substantially shifting the argument to a different level or in a different direction, hoping to develop a consensus, which will enable them to work together in a harmonious and integrated way.

He describes the last as "most consonant with the high moral calling and service commitment of both professions." But he also warns that unless the professions are able to divide up roles in ways that meet the health needs of the population and the budget demands of payers, outsiders will step in to enforce new territorial lines, something that would undermine professional autonomy, power and prestige of the health professions.[9]

The process Dr Baldwin describes is not an easy or quick fix. Dr Jeremy Sturgeon, Director of Medical Oncology at the McGill University Health Centre, participated in a roundtable discussion on nursing in an evolving health system in May 2009. He described physician response to the incorporation of nurse practitioners in oncology at Princess Margaret Hospital in Toronto:

"When the hospital brought in its first nurse practitioner, we oncologists wondered what on earth she would do. Then we learned that she was going to take histories and do physical exams. Again, disbelief! How could she do that? We learned within a few weeks that not only were her histories and physicals more accurate and detailed than those by residents, she brought a new perspective that hadn't ever been included. She told us how the patient and the patient's family felt about what was going on.

The next issue had to do with nurses' notes. It was decided that instead of nurses' notes being on a separate part of the chart, they'd be integrated with the physician notes. This was revolutionary. At first doctors drew a line on the margin beside the physician notes to identify them and skip the nurses' notes. But very quickly, the nurses' notes changed. They no longer just said, 'Had a good day, sat in a chair', and instead became very informative and detailed. Lo and behold, the physicians started reading them, and the lines in the margin of the page went away."[10]

The Surgical Team: No Fumbles Allowed

Veronica D'souza, RN, Matron of the Main Operating Theatre at Bombay Hospital in Mumbai provides a glimpse into the teamwork that takes place in the operating theatre. She appreciates demanding surgeons as they keep her skills honed and enable the team to produce quite miraculous results.

I started my career as a Staff Nurse at the Bombay Hospital in 1980 and worked in all specialties before being promoted to Sister in Charge of Neurosurgery, my favorite area. I had the opportunity to receive special training from renowned neurosurgeons in the UK, Switzerland and Germany. I am currently Matron of the Main Operating Theatre, consisting of seven theatres which has several areas of specialisation, and have had the privilege of assisting the most dynamic and renowned surgeons from India and visiting surgeons from other countries.

Diligence, manual dexterity and careful management of equipment are important in surgical nursing, but so is the ability to empathise with patients and anticipate and provide for their physical and emotional well-being. Operating theatre nurses are generally proud of their role as an assistant to the surgeon and recognise their responsibility to provide the best possible conditions for surgery: asepsis, sterilisation of equipment and instruments, etc..

Surgical nurses must react quickly, observe conscientiously, and have a sound knowledge of anatomy and operative procedures, including the particular techniques of individual surgeons. Surgeons, anesthetists, nurses and theatre attendants are bound into a team. There are stressful moments and tempers can flare but everyone recognises what is at stake and appreciates each other's skills.

Two particular operations stand out in my memory. One involved a first-time mother at 37.5 weeks gestation with a lower segment fibroid that required the surgeon—a very senior obgyn—to deliver the child through a very narrow gap between the uterus and the fibroid. Pediatrician and suction were at the ready as the surgeon opened the uterine wall and delivered the baby by retracting the fibroid to one side. He then removed the 900 gm fibroid without injuring the bladder, checked the uterus for hemorrhage, deposited it back and closed the wound. Tension in the operation room had been very high. The first sigh of relief came when we heard the baby cry. Once the mother was safely off to the recovery room, the surgeon wiped the beads of sweat from his forehead and thanked the operating team with a big smile for the successful surgery.

The other case involved a male patient requiring a left frontal craniotomy for excision of a meningioma. I was a young staff nurse and the surgeon, Dr Suresh Wagh, was a smart, handsome, dynamic personality who had trained at the Guy's Maudsley Hospital in the UK and had very high expectations of the surgical nurses.

The anesthetist induced the patient and handed him over to Dr Wagh, who cleaned and draped exactly as was done in the UK. He would never let us touch the business end of the instrument without a sponge in our hand and hated for us to even turn around while we were assisting him. He would often look over his glasses to see if our attention was still focused. After a bifrontal flap was created along the hairline and the Raney clips were applied the patient started bleeding profusely. There was no time to even look around. Continuous cotton pelgets were passed to the surgeon as he kept cauterising whichever bleeders were seen. There was pin-drop silence as the anaesthetist kept asking for more blood. Once the flap was raised and the dura was opened the patient went into hypotension. Many more units of blood were given. After the meningioma was out, we waited for the bleeding to stop as Dr Wagh caught the remaining bleeders, performed the duraplasty, and closed the wound. The patient was taken to the recovery room, but before we could take a breath, he was rushed back into the operating theatre, pupils dilated. The wound was reopened, the bleeder cauterised, we closed and finally saw him safely off the recovery. This was the most exciting case in my career in the neurosurgery theatre. I enjoyed assisting Dr Wagh and miss him now that he is no longer with us. He certainly kept us on our toes.

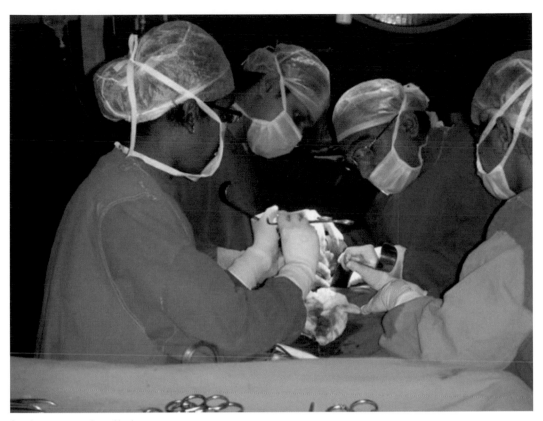

Oncology surgery performed by the oncosurgery team.

Surgeons and scrub nurses come to trust each other's skills and judgment and it is always much more comfortable working with a surgeon who is confident in your abilities. Very often, nurses assist better than the junior residents and they are doing so more often now as surgical residents are shared between two consultants and are not always available. With experience, surgical nurses are able to present the instruments in a fluent motion one after the other and find opportune moments to accomplish what needs to be done without delaying the procedure. Senior nurses share close bonds with the senior consultants and teach the junior nurses how to meet each of their specific requirements.

Surgical nurses today receive specialised training and must become familiar with the new technologies and materials involved in the sophisticated operations we now perform. The work is arduous, especially in very long cardiac, plastic, oncology, neurological and transplant surgeries, but always exciting, with results that were unimaginable until very recently.

There are easier nursing jobs available these days and many young nurses in India are looking for more regular schedules and less stressful caseloads. I, however, have no regrets and am pleased to be able to give my all to the profession. Even during the terror attacks in Mumbai, the OT team under my supervision worked for 48 hours continuously and saved many lives.

Mutual Respect Brings Improvements in Care

Bette Allatt, RN, was head nurse in the neonatal intensive care unit at the Royal Victoria Hospital in Montréal from 1966 until 1993. She identified the ways in which teamwork was promoted through a culture of mutual respect, nursing research and family-centred care. Bette is now retired and living in Calgary.

From day one in the Premature Nursery unit I knew I had joined a family of caregivers. I watched our chief of service sit by a new baby and work with him until he stabilised. As nurses, we worked together with our medical staff and were treated with the utmost respect. Our observations were taken into consideration in daily treatment decisions. We had no residents or interns working in our unit in the early days. The nurses were treated as the important caregivers. We learned to start IV lines with tiny needles designed by our chief and made in our machine shop. We assisted with some of the very first blood exchange transfusions in infants with blood incompatibilities, and had great successes.

Our unit conducted an important study on the oxygen concentration needs for premature babies. Our doctors sat with many a baby with respiratory distress syndrome and adjusted the oxygen according to his colour. The pH values in the babies' blood was closely monitored and adjusted with administration of IV bicarb. It was the start of the era in which we could actually treat respiratory distress syndrome, long before there were even oxygen monitors. Until 1974, we actually had to borrow ventilators from the adult ward and adapt the machines to our tiny patients. When we finally received new ventilators constructed with premmies in mind it was an incredible advancement!

Over my first ten years in the Premmie Nursery, it gradually became a Neonatal Intensive Care Unit or NICU. This specialty branch of pediatrics had been accepted, and residents and medical students were introduced to the unit.

Nursery Research

Research was always an important part of our work, and we were encouraged to look into all aspects of care with a view to making improvements in practice. One challenge was preparing parents to care for their babies when they took them home. In the early years we thought they might contaminate the unit and restricted contact, sending them home with their baby after just two days of rather intensive training. Another nurse and I started a mini-study, visiting the newly discharged babies and parents in their home to assess how well they were coping. As we met with terrified parents who felt they had to keep watch day and night as the nurses had in the NICU, we realised that changes were needed. Parents were thereafter welcomed into the unit and involved with care as much as the fragility of their baby would allow. By the time they brought their baby home they knew about apneic spells, cyanosis, gavage feedings and most of the differences between full term babies and premature babies. They had confidence in their ability to care for their baby. We also arranged for follow-up after discharge.

A research nurse in the unit worked with our chief on defining the characteristics of a premmie. Age could be assessed by features such as foot creases, breast tissue and amount of lanugo and ear lobe tissue. This could all define the gestational age with consideration of the weight and the mother's dates.

We were also conducting research on feeding needs. The number of calories needed for each premmie to grow, what kind of milk—mothers' pumped breast milk, formula, or a combination of both. Different methods of feeding were tested, including intermittent gavage or tube feeding, and constant drip of high caloric formula through an indwelling gastric tube. Parenteral nutrition proved a life-saving method. I understand that our unit was the first to use this formula in Canada. Our chief had gone to Sweden where they were successful in the use of intralipid and protein intravenous solutions to nourish premmies before they could tolerate oral feedings. There was so much going on in improving the quality of care of the tiniest of babies that the interest of all staff was captured.

We lost the fight for some babies' lives, but developed care plans that accorded each death the greatest dignity. Every baby, no matter what gestation or weight, was given a chance to show what effort should be dedicated to extreme life-saving measures. The parents were involved in all decisions and were consulted about the removal

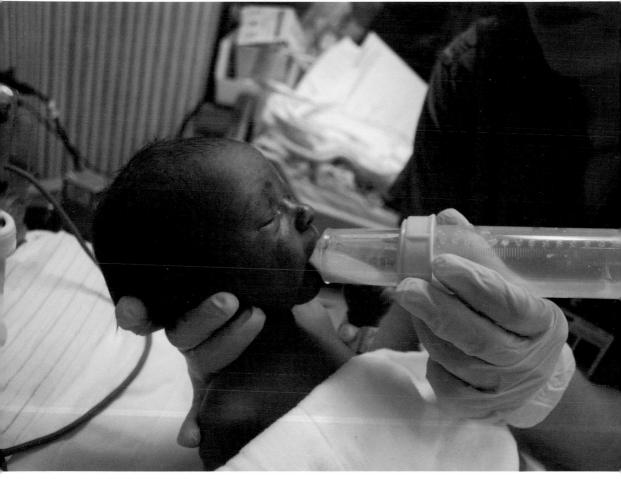

A premature baby being fed by hand.

of life support when things seemed hopeless. We nurses encouraged them to hold their babies as they passed away. We took pictures and gave the parents a lock of hair or small booties their child wore. It was a start for the grieving that followed. Our accomplishment was to help parents accept the situation and help each other.

For a period of time there were multiple applications for every vacancy in the unit. Some of the nurses still working there started back when I first became head nurse in 1966. I stayed in that position until I aged out in 1993. The reason we had such a knowledgeable, devoted and experienced team was that the nursing staff were treated as the first line in the care and management of the babies and their parents. This was long before nurses in other units even hoped for that.

Medical students and residents were taught from day one of their rotation that the nursing staff was to be taken very seriously.

And more was expected of us. We provided introductory talks to each new rotation of doctors and also taught medical students some of the basic treatments that were daily procedures for babies and their families. We earned the respect of most who passed through our unit.

The Team Expands to Include Kangaroo Mothers in Brazil's NICUs

In Brazil, the Ministry of Health began implementing the Kangaroo Mother method in 1999 and it is now widespread in maternity hospitals throughout the country. Neonatologist Dr Ana Lucia Goulart and NICU nurse Flávia Simphronio Balbino recognise how stressful the experience of having a preterm infant can be. The Kangaroo Mother approach to neonatal care aims to see the new baby fully welcomed into the family unit.

The role of the NICU nurse has changed significantly in Brazil, where the Kangaroo Mother Method was adopted in NICUs starting in 1999. The clinical and technical aspects of NICU nursing remain just as important, says Flavia Simphronio Balbino, RN, MScN, Specialist in Neonatal Intensive Care at the Sao Paolo Hospital. "But there is a much greater preoccupation with establishing and strengthening the baby-family bond. It is our job to make sure that the baby's family is comfortable in the NICU. We guide them through the unit, explaining the equipment and encouraging them to touch, hold and talk to their baby. In effect, mothers, and fathers, become part of the care team. They are encouraged to stay with their baby in the NICU as much as possible every day. And the work of the unit adapts to accommodate the family approach." Nurses include mothers in caring for their infants, increasing confidence in their own abilities. Three times a day, the lights in the unit are dimmed for "quiet hour" so mothers can rest or sleep holding their babies in the reclining chairs within the unit, without disturbing vital equipment.

The Kangaroo Mother method was developed as an alternative to incubator care for some premature and low birth weight infants. It was first tried in 1979 by two Colombian neonatologists, Héctor Gómez and Edgar Sanabria, at the Maternal-Infant Institute in Bogotá, as a way to cope with overcrowding and a lack of resources in the NICU. Skin-to-skin contact with the mother replaced incubation. Strapped to the mother's chest 24 hours a day in a specially-designed "pouch", the babies stayed warm and mothers were able to breast feed their infants.

It soon became apparent that the method could also improve outcomes compared to standard NICU care. Benefits included shorter hospital stays, fewer infections, better weight gain, adequate oxygenation, higher and stabilised body temperature, fewer episodes of apnea and less crying. The mothers breastfed more and were more confident monitoring the health of their own babies. From 1984 onwards, the method was widely publicised by UNICEF and adopted at hospitals in many countries.

Flávia Simphronio Balbino, RN, and new mother Mariana da Costa Mariano in the NICU at Sao Paolo Hospital in Brazil.

Interprofessional student group learning a skill from an occupational therapist.

Disaster Management as a Trigger for Interprofessional Collaboration

Professor Yumi Tamura RN CWOCN MSc, of the Kobe Graduate School of Health Sciences and Director of the KIPEC Interprofessional Program at Kobe University, was among three co-authors who introduced the term "interprofessional" to the Japanese nursing lexicon in the late 1990s. At the time, the Japanese term *chi-mu iryou*, or "team-treatment" in English, was not yet the buzzword it is these days. Tamura and her colleagues contributed to defining what the term might mean and how it might be operationalised in Japan. Today, despite lingering vestiges of traditional hierarchy in the relationships between health professionals, more and more healthcare workers share a common understanding of these terms. Increased awareness of the importance of collaborative practice and its education has led to the establishment of JAIPE, the Japan Association for Interprofessional Education. In 2008 approximately ten universities leading the developments in IPE developed this initiative. Another association for collaborative practice has been initiated with partnership of healthcare professional bodies, including nursing.

Modern healthcare in Japan developed on Western modes of practice and medical science. Working relationships between nurses, doctors and other health professionals face similar tensions to those seen in Western countries.

The nurse-doctor relationship has been described as hierarchical.[11] In my experience, the legal phrase of "working under a doctor's instruction" is often interpreted as an order. In Japan, much healthcare is provided in private for-profit clinics where the doctor is also the employer. Nurses can find it very difficult to disagree or raise questions, even when they have doubts about whether a patient is being given the best possible treatment and care. Nurses may simply wait for instructions and become the doctors' handmaiden.[12]

In recent years, however, collaborative practice is increasingly seen as an effective approach to providing high quality, safe and trustworthy medical treatment and care. It is also seen as a way to cope with the challenges inherent in societal changes, the ageing population and the increasing complexity of patients' needs. Further, we have witnessed a drive to shorten hospital stays and provide healthcare in more diverse environments, particularly in patients' homes, and we face a shortage of healthcare professionals, especially doctors. Together, these factors require that nurses' become increasingly multi-skilled and autonomous, which is helping to change the relationship between different health professionals, holding out hope of our becoming equal partners.

Lessons from Disaster Relief

Against this background of gradual change in the relationships between healthcare providers, the experience of coping with natural disasters serves as a powerful accelerant to collaborative practice. In the aftermath of the 1995 Great Hanshin-Awaji Earthquake, Kobe University Hospital was damaged but continued to provide critical care in the aftermath as the main hospital in the disaster region. Hospital staff responded to the needs of earthquake survivors by opening temporary tent clinics that provided some of the most important medical treatment in the area. These tent clinics were often set up near sports halls and schools that had been converted into shelters for the victims.

This response required instant planning, flexibility and above all coordination of activities and resources. Doctors and nurses, including those who were off-duty, reported at the emergency relief headquarters that was set up by the hospital administration. In both the most acute stages, when emergency care and triage were predominantly practiced, as well as in the recovery phase, doctors and nurses worked side by side in equal relationships. Professional roles, boundaries and status moved to the background because the emergency demanded instant responses by whoever was available with matching abilities. Nurses worked autonomously and demonstrated their capacities. Good communication lines were maintained. Tasks at hand were planned and communicated before individuals or small teams set out to execute them. Feedback was provided after completion of these relief management efforts.

A wide range of health professionals pitched in with the immediate relief effort, transporting survivors and assisting in the distribution of basic necessities such as bottled water in the shelters. During these activities, nurses and rehabilitation professionals became aware that the need for

Volunteers and elderly persons participating in recreational exercises at a temporary housing complex.

exercise and activities for disabled people and the frail elderly was not being provided for in the shelters. In response they formed teams and introduced "home" rehabilitation in the shelters and close to temporary homes. In colaboration with lay-person volunteers, they organised programmes to support people's physical and mental health.

The teams that formed in the aftermath of the earthquake demonstrated how much could be accomplished through collaborative practice. The expertise gained was subsequently shared with other regions in Japan and other countries facing natural disasters. Teams from Kobe with different combinations of professionals were dispatched to assist in various efforts. For example, nurse-pharmacist-physician teams were dispatched to Sumatra after the devastating tsunami in Banda-Aceh in 2004. Team members brought together a wide range of professional, language and practical skills, which, along with their shared specialisation of working in disaster relief, allowed them to contribute something useful.

The disaster relief experience has had a lasting impact because it allowed different professional groups to learn about each other and come to value each others' skills. The Ministry of Science and Education in Japan recently stipulated that disaster nursing should be part of pre-qualification nursing education.

The experience following the earthquake in Kobe of working together across professional boundaries of nurses, doctors and other professionals provided the impetus for Kobe University to develop and implement an interprofessional component for the health sciences curriculum.[13]

Collaboration Beyond Disaster Relief

Following five years of planning and trial classes, the health sciences faculty of Kobe University implemented an Interprofessional Education (IPE) programme across the four-year undergraduate curricula for nursing, medical laboratory technique and physical and occupational therapy, with partial participation by students from the school of medicine and the school of pharmacy.[14] In the first year students are introduced to interprofessional basics, which include a client-

Health needs assessment by nurse, doctor and pharmacist.

centred perspective. They learn about modern medicine and bioethics, examining how legal and ethical issues influence healthcare practice and explore the value systems of each profession. Students also experience collaboration in practice. In interprofessional groups of five or six, they visit one of 50 institutions and share their various experiences over a day of presentations.

In their second year, health sciences students are introduced to a wide range of practical topics related to healthcare provision in international and disaster healthcare. In their third year, they undertake healthcare activities in interprofessional groups, looking at the impact of disasters on people's health and well-being, as well as triage and resuscitation during relief efforts. They learn communication and team-building skills as well as problem-identification and problem-solving strategies.

Finally, in their fourth year, students undertake problem-based learning in teams, during which they are required to design interprofessional care and treatment plans in response to a given scenario.

Based on current understanding of what it takes to become interprofessional, particular importance is attached to the following educational goals:

+ Understanding the core concept of 'interprofessional'.

+ Understanding and respecting the roles of different health professions.

+ Acquiring knowledge and skills that can be shared across professional borders.

+ Appreciating the meaning and values of collaboration, and developing a positive attitude toward collaboration.

+ Acquiring skills required for collaboration (leadership, team organisation, problem identification and problem-solving abilities, proposal writing, coordination, and communication skills).

+ Appreciating the reforms needed in health sciences, medical care and welfare from an interprofessional perspective.

In these ways, the IPE programme developed at Kobe University provides an important additional component to traditional specialist education.

Nurses as Architects of Change

Maureen "Shawn" Kennedy, MA, RN is the Editorial Director and interim Editor-in-Chief of *The American Journal of Nursing*, based in New York City. She looks back at some of the American nurses who have played such important roles in social development.

In discussion around American healthcare reform today, few would argue that nurses, despite being the single largest group of healthcare professionals, seem to have little influence on the policies and politics that are shaping how care is delivered. A recent Gallup poll of "executives and thought leaders" commissioned by the Robert Wood Johnson Foundation found that 69 per cent of these leaders felt that nurses were not important decision makers.[15] In fact, in comparison with government officials, insurance and pharmaceutical executives, physicians and patients, nurses were rated the lowest in terms of influence. This is disturbing in that the professionals most present and involved at the point of care seem to have the least influence.

It is also distressing when one thinks that the hospitals and public health we have today stem from processes and systems that were largely developed by nurses. Hospitals still employ organisation and sanitation principles that were set forth by a nurse, Florence Nightingale, after her experience reforming army hospitals during the Crimean War. She knew how to use her position and influence to gain support from high-ranking military and political leaders.

Likewise, the history of healthcare in the US has been marked by nurses. Lillian Wald, together with classmate Mary Brewster, founded the Henry Street Settlement in New York City in 1895 to provide healthcare and teaching to immigrants.[16] This was the beginning of the New York Visiting Nurse Service, the oldest and largest non-profit home health service in the US.[17] Wald was a careful record keeper and tracked data to show the positive outcomes of preventive care. And she used her influence and positive results to persuade wealthy people to support her causes—banker Jacob Schiff donated the house on Henry Street that continues to operate today.[18] In 1902, Wald placed one of her Henry Street nurses in a New York City public school to treat minor conditions so children would not be sent home. After one year, "98 per cent of the children previously excluded for medical reasons are retained."[19]

In 1909, Wald persuaded executives at Metropolitan Life Insurance Company to support her notion that providing visiting nursing services to their policyholders would result in savings by decreasing mortality rates. The experiment worked so well that, by 1911, it was operating in 175 cities in the US and Canada.[20]

In 1915, Lillian D Wald wrote in *The House on Henry Street*: "We soon found that the children's diseases, particularly those of brief duration, lent themselves most advantageously to home treatment. Our records show that in 1914 the Henry Street staff cared for 3,535 cases of pneumonia of all ages, with a mortality rate of 8.05 per cent. For purposes of comparison four large New York hospitals gave us their records of pneumonia during the same period. Their combined figures totaled 1,612, with a mortality rate of 31.2 per cent. Among children under two—the age most susceptible to unfortunate termination of this disorder—the mortality rate from pneumonia in one hospital was 51 per cent, and the average of the four was 38 per cent, while among those of a corresponding age cared for by our nurses it was 9.3 per cent.

Doctors and nurses highly trained in hospital routine are apt to be hospital propagandists until they learn by experience that there is justification for the resistance, on the part of mothers, to the removal of their children to institutions, and that even in homes which, at first glance, it seems impossible to organize in accordance with sick room standards, the little patients' chances for recovery are better than when sent away."[21]

Mary Breckenridge, a nurse midwife, and two colleagues, began the Frontier Nursing Service in Kentucky in 1925. The nurses rode horseback into the mountains, covering 700 square miles, teaching mothers how to care for themselves and their families. Their success in reducing maternal and infant mortality was astounding: between 1925 and 1954, their maternal mortality rate was one-third the rate in the rest of the country (9.1 per 10,000 births compared with 34 per 10,000).[22]

Hospital nursing in the twentieth century was largely based on student servitude in return for training. Nursing practice was proscribed through extensive and specific policy and procedure manuals. Physicians often had the last word on nursing practice. It would be decades before nurses would take charge of their practice within the highly bureaucratic hospital framework.

In the 1960s, the development of critical care units heralded a new era of specialisation and nursing expertise.[23] Loretta Ford teamed-up with physician Henry Silver in 1965 to expand the role of pediatric nurses into pediatric nurse practitioners in the primary care setting.[24] In hospitals, the advanced practice role took the form of clinicians and clinical nurse specialists.[25] Other innovations included Lydia Hall's nurse-led Loeb Center for Nursing and Rehabilitation in 1963, where nursing occupied centre stage and medicine was ancillary.[26] But it was not until 1969 when Marie Manthey successfully introduced primary nursing in a Minnesota hospital that hospital nursing began to widely embrace a professional practice model in which nurses assumed 24-hour accountability for their patients.[27] Margaret Sanger advocated for women's reproductive rights in the 1920s and later helped found Planned Parenthood. Hildegarde Peplau pioneered the interpersonal techniques that serve as the underpinnings of psychiatric and mental health nursing today.

In more recent history, we can look to Ruth Lubic, a nurse-midwife who implemented two free-standing childbirth centres in New York City and then the Family Health and Birth Center in Washington, DC. Lubic has proven that nurse-midwives can provide safe, cost-effective, high quality care managing childbirth outside the hospital. The costs of childbirth at the Manhattan Childbirth Center, which opened in 1975, were one-quarter to one-half of the cost for delivery in private hospitals.[28] When critics charged that her outcomes would not be the same in a low-income area, she opened a centre in 1988 in the South Bronx and achieved similar results. In 1993, she received a MacArthur Genius Award and used the funds towards opening the facility in the nation's capitol. Lubic says that facility has "half as many cesarean sections, preterm births, and low-birth-weight neonates as those in the rest of the city", and she estimates her centre saves the city over $1 million annually.[29]

Mary Naylor, a nurse specialising in care for older adults, researched what happens when vulnerable elderly patients move from one care setting to another. Since 1989, Naylor and colleagues at the University of Pennsylvania have developed a model of transitional care, using advanced practice nurses to manage the care of high-risk older adults with various medical and surgical conditions as they transition from hospital to home. Their system of protocol-driven clinical management with ongoing care and follow-up visits and phone calls has proven to reduce rehospitalisations and costs.[30] It is being considered by the Centers for Medicare and Medicaid as a model for transitional care.[31]

Many states prohibit qualified nurse practitioners, nurse anesthetists and nurse-midwives from fully practicing within their scope unless there is a physician supervisor or partner, despite myriad studies which show these advanced practitioners deliver quality and cost-effective care as independent practitioners.[32] It is critical, as efforts are made to redesign the US healthcare system, rein in costs, and improve safety, access and quality, that nurses be allowed to practice to the full extent of their capabilities. And it is not just nurses who feel this way. The Gallup Poll referred to at the beginning of this essay found that while the majority of respondents did not feel nurses were influencing health reform, 92 per cent of these opinion leaders felt that nurses should have "a great deal" of influence. The issue is whether nurses, and these leaders, will be heard.

Candice Pellett speaking at the launch of the Transformational Guides at the Department of Health, 2009.

A Change for the Better

Candice Pellett is a District Nurse in the UK. She works in clinical practice as a Case Manager, and is currently seconded to the Department of Health as Clinical Lead Nurse on the Transforming Community Services programme. Candice began her career as an auxiliary nurse in 1987, starting her nurse training in Lincolnshire in 1992, and qualifying in 1995 with a Diploma in Adult Nursing.

"I started work on the Oncology ward in the hospital where I trained; within four months I had secured a job as a community staff nurse in Bourne, Lincolnshire. In 1998 I was awarded a secondment to undertake a BSc degree pathway to train as a District Nurse, and I started work as a District Nurse back in Bourne in 1999. I spent over two years as a Lecturer/ Practitioner, teaching mainly pre-registration nursing students at Nottingham University."

Nursing is Candice's second career. After leaving school, she worked in a bank. When she was pregnant with her first child she left banking and, as she had always been interested in nursing, she started work as a nursing auxiliary on an ad-hoc basis when her children were young. Finding that she loved it, she started nurse training when her youngest child was seven years old.

"I wasn't sure at that stage what I wanted from nursing but I saw it as a challenge. Training to be a nurse is very different from learning at school age. As a nursing student, you need to be very disciplined and motivated as there is a lot of self-directed study. My cohort encountered some hostility from the trained staff on the wards, as we were only the second group to start a diploma course, and many misunderstood what the course was about.

I think nursing has changed for the better since I started my nursing career. We have more responsibility—I am now an Independent Prescriber so can deliver holistic care to my patients following diagnosis (within my competence). There is also a lot of training available for nurses, which opens up further career opportunities.

My career has delivered more than I would have thought possible, and I love every part of it. Since being awarded the 'Queen's Nurse' title nearly three years ago, I have had countless opportunities to broaden my knowledge with the support of the Queen's Nursing Institute."

In her work as a District Nurse, Candice cares for palliative and end-of-life patients as well as patients with long-term conditions. She is also responsible for teaching the pre-registration nursing students and trained nurses placed in her team who are following a degree pathway in District Nursing. Her secondment at the Department of Health means that she is involved with promoting the six Transformational Guides (health and well-being and reducing health inequalities; children, young people and families; acute care closer to home; long-term conditions; rehabilitation services and end of life care) that were published in 2009, looking at how they are being embedded into clinical practice throughout England.[33]

"The demands on community teams have risen considerably over the past decade with 90 per cent of people who access healthcare doing so in primary and community settings. The six best practice guides have been developed in conjunction with committed and experienced health professionals and are tools that highlight a number of actions that can make a real difference to patients' lives."

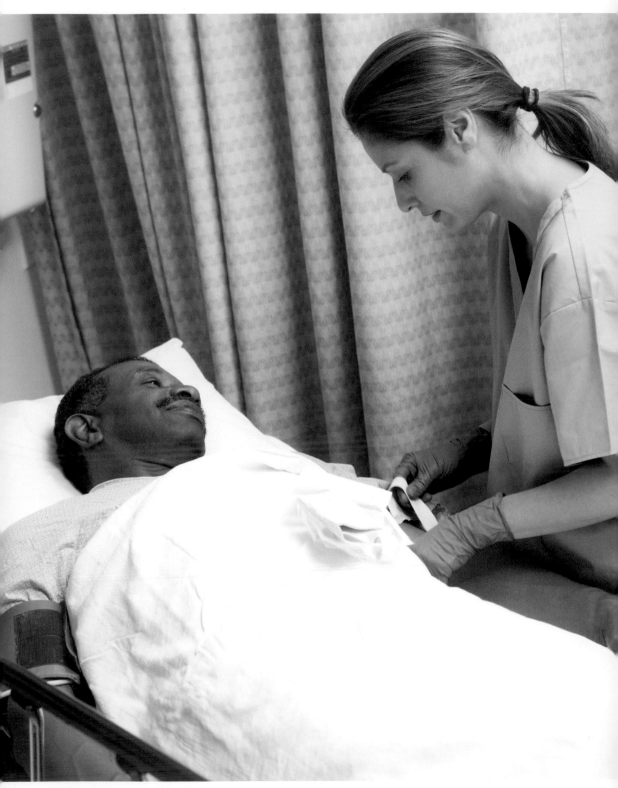

A nurse caring for a patient at his bedside.

A Return to Dignity

In the UK, the Royal College of Nursing is re-emphasising the notion of dignity in caring. "The provision of dignified care is at the very heart of nursing. There are many opportunities for nurses to promote dignified care, but there are also challenges."

When dignity is absent from care, people feel devalued, lacking control and comfort. They may also lack confidence, be unable to make decisions and feel humiliated, embarrassed and ashamed. Providing dignity in care centres on three integral aspects: respect, compassion and sensitivity. This means:

+ Respecting patients' and clients' diversity and cultural needs; their privacy—including protecting it as much as possible in large, open-plan hospital wards; and the decisions they make.

+ Being compassionate when a patient or client and/or their relatives need emotional support, rather than just delivering technical nursing care.

+ Demonstrating sensitivity to patients' and clients' needs, ensuring their comfort.

The RCN aims to highlight that dignity is the essence of nursing care and should be at the heart of everything nurses do.[34] As a part of the Dignity Campaign, over 2,000 nurses told the RCN about their experiences and attitudes to dignity. The survey found that:

+ More than eight out of ten respondents feel that they always or sometimes feel upset or distressed because they are unable to give the dignified care they know they should.

+ 65 per cent say they sometimes or never have enough time to devote to the dignity of their patients or clients.

+ Meanwhile more than 98 per cent say that the dignity of their patients and clients is important to them.

Looking at the physical environment, several issues prevent dignified care being given:

+ Overcrowded wards and the layout of the clinical area.

+ The curtains around beds.

+ Noisy and disruptive environments.

+ Mixed sex wards.[35]

Nurses feel that resources and staffing levels, overwhelming paperwork, targets and statistics and a lack of leadership on this issue stand in the way of giving dignified care. The Dignity Campaign continues to be a very successful campaign, and is now being rolled out and managed in RCN countries and regions.[36]

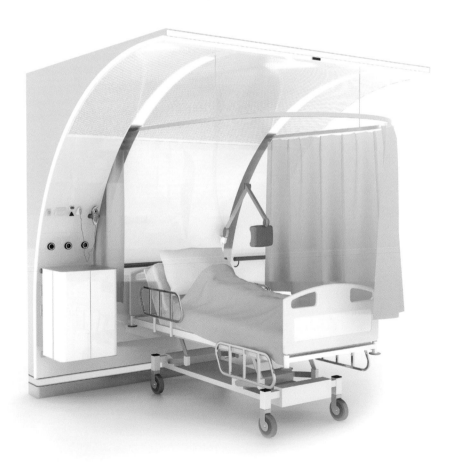

Modular bed pod by Nightingale Associates/Billings Jackson Design. This bed system with its modesty screens, improved acoustics, lighting and additional storage, gives patients more control over their environment. It could be rapidly installed in hospitals, enabling them to quickly convert under-used space into single bed spaces without the need for major refurbishment.

As a nurse, I know that patients expect and deserve not only high quality, safe and effective care, but a dignified experience when they go into hospital. It is essential that the high standard of work carried out by our skilled NHS staff is not undermined by patients feeling vulnerable and undignified when they receive treatment.

Ann Keen, UK Health Minister.

Universal gown by Ben de Lisi. This one-size-fits-all gown is reversible, with a choice of v-neck or round-neck. It is easy to put on and covers the patient's front and back, while its press-stud fastenings mean equipment like IV lines can be attached without exposing the skin.

Design for Patient Dignity

The Department of Health teamed up with the Design Council to bring together some of the best minds in the design industry with those working on the frontline in the NHS. Seven teams of leading UK product, interiors, fashion and systems designers, architects and manufacturers were appointed to work on an exciting range of briefs to help to improve the hospital environment and patient experience.

The teams worked intensively with patients, experts, hospital staff and others to make some of their ideas a reality and to develop prototypes, with the eventual aim of introducing the designs into UK hospitals. They responded to briefs that addressed issues including how to deliver same-sex accommodation in existing NHS hospitals, how to provide a range of functional patient clothes that allow for greater dignity, and how to create a more dignified toileting and washing experience in hospitals.

We believe that nurses and midwives have key and increasingly important roles to play in society's efforts to tackle the public health challenges of our time, as well as in ensuring the provision of high-quality, accessible, equitable, efficient and sensitive health services which ensure continuity of care and address people's rights and changing needs.

Munich Declaration: Nurses and midwives: a Force for Health, 2000

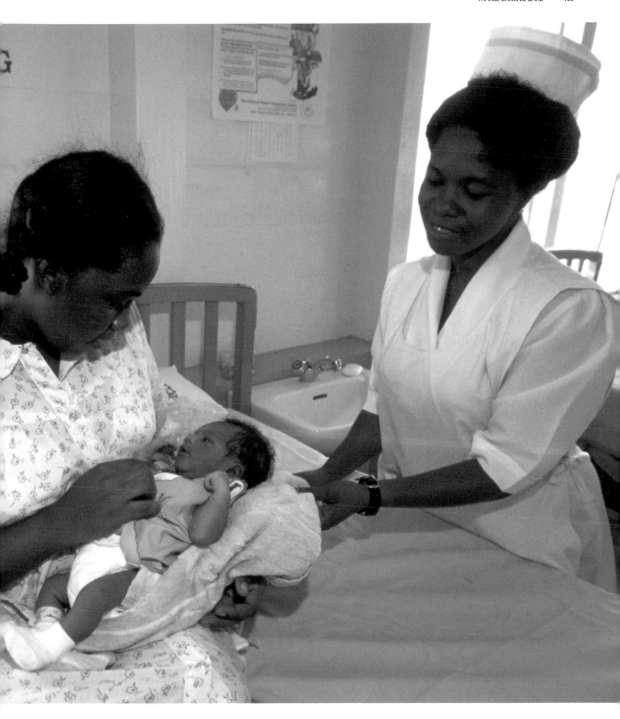

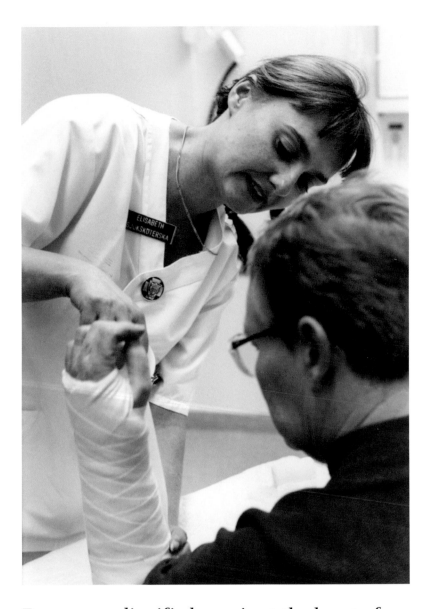

For nurses, dignified care is at the heart of everything they do. Offering high standards of care can be a challenge, but a desire to offer it to patients is something that unites all nurses. As we address public health challenges and, as more people in the ageing population live with long-term conditions, compassionate nursing care is crucial.

Janet Davies, Executive Director of Nursing and Service Delivery, Royal College of Nursing.

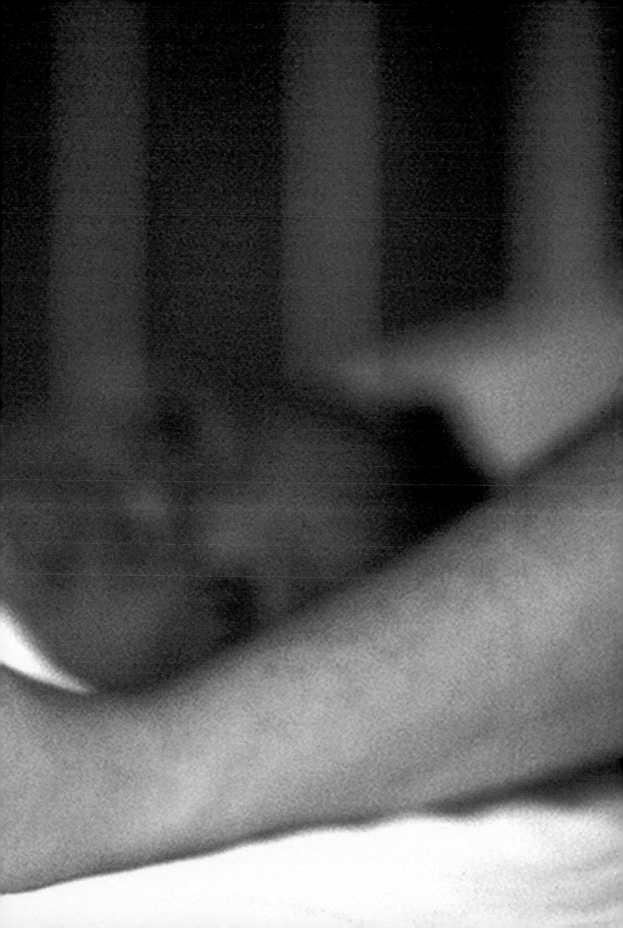

Further Reading

Abel-Smith, B, *A History of the Nursing Profession*, London: Heinemann, 1960.

Advice to Trusts on the main components of the design brief for healthcare buildings, NHS Estates, 2002.

Aiken, L and A Cheung, *Nurse Workforce Challenges in the United States: Implications for policy*, Paris: OECD Health Working Paper No. 35, 2008.

Alalouch, C and P Aspinall, "Spatial attributes of hospital multi-bed wards and preferences for privacy", *Facilities*, vol. 25, no 9/10, 2007, Emerald Group Publishing Limited.

Baldwin, D, "Some historical notes on interdisciplinary and interprofessional education and practice in health care in the USA", *Journal of Interprofessional Care*, vol. 10, no 2,1996, Republished in *Journal of Interprofessional Care*, vol. 21, no. 1, October 2007.

Baly, M, *Nursing and Social Change*, London: Heinemann, 1980.

Barr, H, "Interprofessional education: The fourth focus", *Journal of Interprofessional Care*, vol. 21, no. 2, 2007.

Bates, C, "A caring profession: centuries of nursing in Canada", *Canadian Medical Association Journal* vol. 173, no. 3, 2 August 2005.

Bates, C, *On All Frontiers: Four centuries of Canadian nursing*, Ottawa: University of Ottawa Press and Canadian Museum of Civilization, 2005.

Baumann, A and J Blythe, "Globalization of Higher Education in Nursing", *Online Journal of Issues in Nursing*, vol. 13, no. 2, 2008.

Bostridge, M, *Florence Nightingale, the Woman and her Legend*, London: Viking, 2008.

Buchan, J, *The Global Shortage of Registered Nurses: An overview of issues and actions*, Geneva: International Council of Nurses, 2004.

Crowther, A, S McGann, and R Dougall, *A History of the Royal College of Nursing 1916–90. A Voice for Nurses*, Manchester: Manchester University Press, 2009.

Currie, M, *Fever hospitals and fever nurses: a British social history of fever nursing: a national service*, London: Routledge, 2005.

Darbyshire, P and S Gordon, "Exploring Popular Images and Reputations of Nurses and Nursing" In J Daly, et al., ed. *Professional Nursing: Concepts, Issues, and Challenges.* New York: Springer Publishing Company, 2005.

Department of Health White Paper, "Health System Transformation", *South African Government Gazette* No 17910, Government Department of Health, 16 April 1997.

Digby, A, *Diversity and Division in Medicine. Health care in South Africa from the 1800s*, Oxford: Peter Lang, 2006.

Dingwall, R, AM Rafferty and C Webster, *An Introduction to the Social History of Nursing*, London: Routledge, 1988.

Fairman, J, "Distribution of intensive care facilities in the British Isles", *Care of the Critically Ill* vol. 2, no. 5, November 1986.

Fairman, J and P D'Antonio, "Virtual power: gendering the nurse-technology relationship", *Nursing Inquiry*, vol. 6, 12 May 1999.

Francis, S and R Glanville, *Building a 2020 vision: Future healthcare environments*, The Stationery Office, 2001.

Frontline Care, Report by the Prime Minister's Commission on the Future of Nursing and Midwifery in England, 2010, London: The Prime Minister's Commission on the Future of Nursing and Midwifery in England, 2010.

Godden, J, *Lucy Osburn, a lady displaced*, Sydney: Sydney University Press, 2006.

Guenther, R and G Vittori, *Sustainable Healthcare Architecture*, Hoboken: John Wiley and Sons, 2008.

Haggard, L and S Hosking, *Healing the Hospital Environment*, London: Routledge, 1999.

Hallett, C, *Celebrating Nurses*, New York: Barron's Educational Series, August 2010.

Hallett, C, *Containing Trauma: Nursing Work in the First World War*, Manchester: Manchester University Press, 2010.

Helmstadter, C, "Early Nursing Reform in Nineteenth-Century London: A Doctor-Driven Phenomenon", *Medical History* vol. 46, 2002.

Henderson, V, *Principles and Practice of Nursing*, London: Macmillan, 1978.

Henderson, V, *The Nature of Nursing*, New York: Macmillan Publishing, 1966.

Hertzler, AA, "Florence Nightingale's Influence on Civil War Nutrition" in *Nutrition Today*, vol. 39, no. 4, July/August 2004.

High Quality Care for All: Our Journey So Far, Department of Health, 2009.

Hudson Jones, A, *Images of Nurses: Perspectives from History, Art and Literature*, Philadelphia: University of Pennsylvania Press, 1988.

James, PW and W Tatton-Brown, *Hospitals: Design and Development*, London: The Architectural Press, 1986.

Jaret, P, *Nurse: A World of Care*, Atlanta: Emory University, 2008.

Keeling, A, "Herbal Medicines in the Kentucky Mountains: the frontier nursing service, 1925–1950" *Windows in Time*, vol. 11, no. 2, 2003.

Kennedy, MS, "In Memoriam: Imogene King, December 24 2007", *The American Journal of Nursing*, vol. 108, no. 3, March 2008.

Kingma, M, *Nurses on the Move: Migration and the Global Health Care Economy*, Cambridge: Cornell University Press, 2006.

Malkin, J, *Hospital Interior Architecture: Creating Healing Environments for Special Patient Populations*, New York: Van Nostrand Rienhold, 1992.

McGann, S, *The Battle of the Nurses'*, London: Scutari Press, 1992.

Monk, T, *Hospital Builders,* Great Britain: Wiley-Academy, 2004.

Nickl-Weller, C and Hans Nickl, *Masterpieces: Hospital Architecture and Design*, Salenstien: Verlagshaus Braun, 2009.

Nightingale, F, *Notes on Nursing: What it is, and what it is not*, New York: D. Appleton and Company, 1860.

Nightingale, F, *Notes on Hospitals,* London: Longman, Green, Longman, Roberts and Green, 1863.

Noble, A, S Francis, R Glanville and P Scher, *50 Years of ideas in health care buildings*, London: The Nuffield Trust, 1999.

Prasad, S ed., *Changing Hospital Architecture*, RIBA Publishing, 2008.

Radical improvements in hospital design: Healthy Hospitals campaign report, London: Commission for Architecture and the Built Environment, 2003.

Rafferty, AM, J Robinson and R Elkan, eds., *Nursing History and the Politics of Welfare*, London: Routledge, 1997.

Rafferty, AM, *The Politics of Nursing Knowledge*, London: Routledge, 1996.

Risse, GB, *Mending Bodies, Saving Souls: A History of Hospitals*, New York City: Oxford University Press, 1999.

Rogers, ME, *An Introduction to the Theoretical Basis of Nursing*, Philadelphia: FA Davis, 1989.

Rosenfield, Z and I Rosenfield, *Hospital Architecture and Beyond*, New York: Van Nostrand Reinhold, 1969.

Romanow, R, (commissioner) Commission on the Future of Health Care in Canada, *Building on Values: The Future of Health Care in Canada: Final Report*, Ottawa: Government of Canada, 2002.

Schmitt, M, "Collaboration improves the quality of care: methodological challenges and evidence from US health care research", *Journal of Interprofessional Care*, vol. 15, no. 1, 2001.

Schorr, TM and MS Kennedy, et al., *100 Years of American Nursing*, Philadelphia: Lipncott, 1999.

Seacole, M, *Wonderful Adventures of Mrs. Seacole in Many Lands*, London: James Blackwood, 1857.

Stevens, R, *In Sickness and In Wealth: American Hospitals in the Twentieth Century*, Baltimore: The John Hopkins University Press, 1999.

Stewart, Dr R, *Leading in the NHS*, Basingstoke: Macmillan, 1989.

Sweet, H and R Dougall, *Community Healthcare and Primary Healthcare in Twentieth Century Britain*, London/New York: Routledge, 2007.

Sweet, H, *To Investigate the Creation and Subsequent Development of ICUs in the United Oxford Hospitals in the context of ICU development elsewhere in the UK*, MA Dissertation, Oxford Brookes University, 1994.

Sweet, H, "Putting South African professional nursing on the world map: Sister Henrietta Stockdale, 1847–1911", *Journal of the South African Theatre Nurse Organisation* Special Anniversary Issue December 2005.

Sweet, H, "Expectations, Encounters and Ecclesiastics: Mission Medicine in Zululand" in: M Harrison, M Jones and H Sweet eds. *From Western Medicine to Global Medicine: The Hospital Beyond the West*, Hyderabad: Orient Longman, 2009.

Takahashi, A, *The Development of the Japanese Nursing Profession: Adopting and Adapting Western Influences*, London: Routledge, 2003.

Tschudin, V and AJ Davis, eds., *The Globalisation of Nursing*, Abingdon: Radcliffe Publishing Ltd, 2008.

Thomas, P, "The international migration of Indian nurses", *International Nursing Review*, vol. 53, 2006.

The role of hospital design in the recruitment, retention and performance of NHS nurses in England: Full Report, PricewaterhouseCoopers LLP, in association with the University of Sheffield and Queen Margaret University College, Edinburgh for CABE, London: Commission for Architecture and the Built Environment, 2004.

The role of hospital design in the recruitment, retention and performance of NHS nurses in England: Full Report Appendices, PricewaterhouseCoopers LLP, in association with the University of Sheffield and Queen Margaret University College, Edinburgh for CABE, London: Commission for Architecture and the Built Environment, 2004.

The role of hospital design in the recruitment, retention and performance of NHS nurses in England: Executive Summary, PricewaterhouseCoopers LLP, in association with the University of Sheffield and Queen Margaret University College, Edinburgh for CABE, London: Commission for Architecture and the Built Environment, 2004.

Tomey, AM and MR Alligood, *Nursing Theorists and Their Work*, 4th ed. Boston: Mosby, 1998.

Ulrich, R and C Zimring, *The role of the physical environment in the hospital of the 21st century: a once in-a-lifetime opportunity*, The Center for Health Design, 2004.

Ulrich, R, "A view through a window may influence recover from surgery", *Science,* vol. 224, 1984.

Verderber, SF and BJ Refuerzo, *Innovations in Hospice Architecture*, London: Taylor and Francis, 2006.

Verderber, S, *Innovations in Hospital Architecture*, Routledge, 2010.

Versluysen, MC, "Old Wives' Tales? Women Healers in English History", C Davies, ed. *Rewriting Nursing History*, London: Croom Helm, 1982.

Wagenaar, C ed., *The Architecture of Hospitals*, Amsterdam: Nai Uitgevers Pub, 2006.

Wanless, D, *Securing our Future Health: Taking a Long-Term View*, London: HM Treasury, 2002.

Wells, H, *Chief Nurse*, Grosset and Dunlap, 1944.

West Wing: Making art and architecture work for health, Barts and The London NHS Trust, 2005.

World Health Organization, *The World Health Report 2006: Working together for health*, Geneva: WHO, 2006.

Worpole, K, *Modern Hospice Design*, London: Routledge, 2009.

End Notes

What is a Nurse?

1. In the UK, hospitals and by implication, nursing reform, were linked to Poor Law and Workhouse reform and followed a series of Parliamentary Acts beginning with the Poor Law Amendment Act of 1834, but gathering momentum in the 1850s as demand for trained nurses increased. The early phases were largely doctor-led—see: Carol Helmstadter (2002) 'Early Nursing Reform in Nineteenth-Century London: A Doctor-Driven Phenomenon' *Medical History* 46: 325–350. This need was underlined by the high mortality of injured during the Crimean War. However, the movement also reflected reform happening elsewhere in Europe.

2. See for example: Godden, Judith, *Lucy Osburn, a lady displaced*, (Sydney: Sydney University Press, 2006); H Sweet, (2005) 'Putting South African professional nursing on the world map: Sister Henrietta Stockdale, 1847–1911' in: *Journal of the South African Theatre Nurse Organisation*, Special Anniversary Issue December 2005, pp. 50–54—both Lucy Osborne and Sister Henrietta were trained in London hospitals and took many of Nightingale's ideas learned there to Australia and South Africa respectively; See: Takahashi, A, *The Development of the Japanese Nursing Profession: Adopting and Adapting Western Influences,* London: Routledge, 2003; For example, see: Hertzler, Ann A, 'Florence Nightingale's Influence on Civil War Nutrition' in *Nutrition Today:* 39:4 July/August 2004, pp. 157–160.

3. See: McGann, Susan, 'The Battle of the Nurses', London: Scutari Press, 1992; Dingwall, R, AM Rafferty, and C Webster, *An Introduction to the Social History of Nursing,* London: Routledge,1988, consider the role of the informal carer or amateur nurse—often consigned to being the remnants of 'pre-industrial nursing', and the techniques carried out by them as do H Sweet, with R Dougall, *Community Healthcare and Primary Healthcare in Twentieth Century Britain,* London/New York: Routledge, 2007; see also: Abel-Smith, B, *A History of the Nursing Profession,* London: Heinemann, 1960.

4. Crowther, A, S McGann, R Dougall, *A Voice for Nurses; a History of the Royal College of Nursing*

1916–90, Manchester: Manchester University Press, 2009.

5. South Africa instituted registration in the Cape in 1891 under the Medical Act No.34 (1891) but this was ultimately under medical regulation; In September 1901 the Nurses' Registration Act was passed in New Zealand, providing for the registration of trained nurses. The legislation came into effect on 1 January 1902, leading New Zealand to become the first country in the world to regulate nurses nationally under Nursing regulation.

6. North Carolina, New Jersey, New York and Virginia all achieved state registration within months of each other in 1903.

7. In South Australia the Nurses Registration Act was passed in 1920 with Western Australia following suite the following year. Victoria passed its nursing registration act two years later, in 1923.

8. Unmarried status was, for the most part, an unwritten rule which was gradually eroded so that by mid-century it applied largely only to nurses in training in most countries.

9. For example, in the UK the Midwives' Acts of 1902 which established a Roll (national register) of midwives, and the Maternity and Child Welfare Act of 1918 which gave legal recognition to the child welfare services that had developed after the 1907 Notification of Births Act; In particular the Local Government Acts of 1929 and 1963; The Education Act of 1870 was seen as a turning point for women's higher education.

10. In doing so this reduced the strain on voluntarily run district nursing associations, enabling them to broaden their remit to a wider public and thereby increasing the nurses' workload substantially.

11. On 5 July 1948 the National Health Service took control of 480,000 hospital beds in England and Wales. An estimated 125,000 nurses and 5,000 consultants were available to care for hospital patients. http://www.nursingtimes.net/the-birth-of-the-nhs-july-5th-1948/441954.article; The 1949 Nurses' Act amended the constitution of the GNC establishing nurse training committees for each of the 14 Regional Hospital Boards set up by the NHS Act. It also amalgamated the general and male nurse parts of the Nursing Register and closed other supplementary parts.

12. For example, The University of Minnesota bestowed the first bachelors degree in nursing in 1909, whilst the first university based nursing school to appear in Canada was established in 1919 by the University of British Columbia, in Vancouver.

13. See for example: Fairman, Julie and Pat D'Antonio, 'Virtual power: gendering the nurse-technology relationship' *Nursing Inquiry* 12 May 1999; 6:178–186; Sweet, H and R Dougall, *Community Healthcare and Primary Healthcare in Twentieth Century Britain* pp. 135–150.

14. Nurses Act 1943 (Section 1(2)) Enrolled nurses were similar to Licensed Practical or Vocational Nurses in the USA and registered practical nurses in Canada.

15. This is detailed in: Currie, M, *Fever hospitals and fever nurses : a British social history of fever nursing : a national service,* London: Routledge, 2005.

16. 'Specialling' was a nursing term widely used to describe the intensive nursing care provided to critically ill patients, usually in a side-ward or especially designated area of the main medical or surgical ward by more experienced nurses. It pre-dated the concept of 'Intensive Care' or 'Intensive Therapy', 'Coronary Care' etc. in which the hospital's most critically ill patients were all cared for in one ward, by nurses trained in that specialty; This development is explored in Fairman, J, 'Distribution of intensive care facilities in the British Isles' *Care of the Critically Ill* 2 November 1986, p. 5; and Sweet, H, *To Investigate the Creation and Subsequent Development of ICUs in the United Oxford Hospitals in the context of ICU development elsewhere in the UK.* MA Dissertation, Oxford Brookes University (1994): See for example: Keeling, Arlene 'Herbal Medicines in the Kentucky Mountains: the frontier nursing service, 1925–1950', *Windows in Time*, Volume 11, Issue 2, 2003 pp. 6–8: Bates, Christina 'A caring profession: centuries of nursing in Canada', *Canadian Medical Association Journal* 2 August 2005; 173(3): pp. 288–289; Sweet, H, (2009). 'Expectations, Encounters and Ecclesiastics: Mission Medicine in Zululand' in: Harrison, Mark, Margaret Jones and Helen Sweet (eds.) *From Western Medicine to Global Medicine: The Hospital Beyond the West* (Hyderabad: Orient Longman): p. 344.

17. See for example: Keeling, Arlene 'Herbal Medicines in the Kentucky Mountains: the frontier nursing service, 1925–1950', *Windows in Time*, Volume 11, Issue 2, 2003 pp. 6–8; Bates, Christina 'A caring profession: centuries

of nursing in Canada' *Canadian Medical Association Journal* 2005 August 2; 173(3): pp. 288–289; Sweet, H, (2009). 'Expectations, Encounters and Ecclesiastics: Mission Medicine in Zululand' in: Harrison, Mark, Margaret Jones and Helen Sweet (eds.) *From Western Medicine to Global Medicine: The Hospital Beyond the West* (Hyderabad: Orient Longman): p. 344.

18. After the Second World War, men were accepted by the Queen's Nursing Institute for training as district nurses. In general, men were entering the profession in far greater number after the Second World War with many rising rapidly to the better paid teaching and administrative posts—see: Crowther, A, S McGann, R Dougall, *A Voice for Nurses; a History of the Royal College of Nursing 1916-90*: pp. 197–203; See: Sweet, H, with Dougall, R, *Community Healthcare and Primary Healthcare in Twentieth Century Britain.*

19. For a more detailed discussion see: Digby, Anne, *Diversity and Division in Medicine. Health care in South Africa from the 1800s* (Oxford: Peter Lang, 2006). pp. 229–276; Sweet, H, (2009). 'Expectations, Encounters and Ecclesiastics': pp. 330–359; *White Paper on Health System Transformation*, Issued by: Government Department of Health 16 April 1997, published in *South African Government Gazette*, No 17910.

20. ICN, 2001b, Constitution, Article 6. http://www.icn.ch/matters_credentialing.htm

21. Baumann, A, 2004, The International Nursing Labour Market Report, http://www.cna-nurses.ca/CNA/documents/pdf/publications/International_Nursing_Labour_Market_e.pdf

22. Castledine, G, *British Journal of Nursing*, Vol 18 No. 22, 2009.

23. AACN report on 2008–2009 Enrollment and Graduations in Baccalaureate and Graduate Programs in Nursing.

24. Bureau of Labor Statistics, US Department of Labor, *Occupational Outlook Handbook, 2010–11 Edition*, http://www.bls.gov/oco/ocos083.htm.

25. Mussallem, HK, *Spotlight on nursing education: Pilot project for the evaluation of schools of nursing in Canada,* Canadian Nurses' Association, Ottawa: 1960. For more on Dr Mussallem's contribution to nursing in Canada and internationally see the Dr HK, Mussallem, *Biography Project,* www.drhkm.ca.

26. International Council of Nurses, *The scope of practice, standards and competencies of the advanced practice nurse,* Geneva: 2008.

27. American Nurses Association, *Nursing: Scope and standards of practice*. Washington, DC: 2004; Royal College of Nursing, *Defining nursing*, 2003. http://www.rcn.org.uk/__data/assets/pdf_file/0003/78564/001983.pdf.

28. Baumann, A and B Silverman, "The ethics of the new economy: Restructuring and beyond: De-professionalization in health care." In L Groake (ed.), *Flattening the Hierarchy* (pp. 203–211). Waterloo, Ontario: Wilfred Laurier University Press, 1998.

29. Baumann, A and J Blythe, "Globalization of higher education in nursing", *The Online Journal of Issues in Nursing*, 13(2), 2008. http://www.nursingworld.org/MainMenuCategories/ANAMarketplace/ANAPeriodicals/OJIN/TableofContents/vol132008/No2Mayo8/Globalizationof HigherEducation.aspx

30. Baumann, A and J Blythe, "Globalization of higher education in nursing", *The Online Journal of Issues in Nursing*, 13(2), 2008. http://www.nursingworld.org/MainMenuCategories/ANAMarketplace/ANAPeriodicals/OJIN/TableofContents/vol132008/No2Mayo8/Globalizationof HigherEducation.aspx

31. Baumann, A and J Blythe, "Globalization of higher education in nursing", *The Online Journal of Issues in Nursing*, 13(2), 2008. http://www.nursingworld.org/MainMenuCategories/ANAMarketplace/ANAPeriodicals/OJIN/TableofContents/vol132008/No2Mayo8/Globalizationof HigherEducation.aspx; Benelux Bologna Secretariat, *About the Bologna Process*. http://www.ond.vlaanderen.be/hogeronderwijs/bologna/about/.

32. Baumann, A and J Blythe, "Nursing human resources: Human cost versus human capital in the restructured health care system." *Health Perspectives* 3(1), pp. 27–34, 2003.

33. Zena Edmund-Charles' full story, http://www.districtnursing150.org.uk/stories_zena_edmund-charles.htm

Passport to the World

1. IOM. (2005). World migration 2005: Costs and benefits of international migration. Geneva: International Organization for Migration. UN. (2006). International migration facts and figures. www.un.org/esa/population/hldmigration/Text/Migration_factsheet.pdf

2. Zlotnik H, (2003). The global dimensions of female migration. Migration Information Source, Migration Policy Institute (MPI) Washington DC, USA. www.migrationinformation.org/Feature/display.cfm?id=109

3. Timur, S, (2000). Changing trends and major issues in international migration: An overview of the UNESCO programmes. International Migration 165: pp. 255–269. New York, USA: Center for Migration Studies.

4. IOM. (2003). World migration 2003: Managing migration—Challenges and responses for people on the move. Geneva: International Organization for Migration.

5. UN. (2006). International migration facts and figures. www.un.org/esa/population/hldmigration/Text/Migration_factsheet.pdf

6. Stilwell, B, K Diallo, P Zurn, MR Dal Poz, O Adams and J Buchan, (2003). Developing evidence-based ethical policies on the migration of health workers: Conceptual and practical challenges. Human Resources for Health 1(8), pp. 1–19; ICN/FNIF. (2006). The global nursing shortage: Priority areas for intervention. Geneva: International Council of Nurses; WHO. (2006). The world health report 2006—Working together for health. Geneva: World Health Organization.

7. Kingma, M, (2006). Nurses on the move: Migration and the global health care economy. Ithaca: Cornell University Press.

8. WHO. (2006). The world health report 2006—Working together for health. Geneva: World Health Organization.

9. Artigot, F, (2003). "Les hôpitaux canadiens battent le rappel des infirmières québécoises exilées in Suisse." *Le Temps*, 17 October.

10. An Bord Altranis. Registration information 2005. www.nursingboard.ie.

11. Martineau, T, K Decker and P Bundred (2002). Briefing note on international migration of health professionals: Leveling the playing field for developing country health systems. Liverpool: Liverpool School of Tropical Medicine.

12. Opiniano, JM (2002). Over 100 Pinoy nurses exploited in UK private nursing homes. http://cyberdyaryo.com/features/f2002_0325_04.htm

13. Buchan, J, R Jobanputra, P Gough and R Hutt (2005). Internationally recruited nurses in London: Profile and implications for policy. London: King's Fund.

14. WHO. (2006). The world health report 2006—Working together for health. Geneva: World Health Organization.

15. Dugger, C (2006). US plan to lure nurses may hurt poor nations. *New York Times*, 24 May;

WHO. (2006). The world health report 2006—Working together for health. Geneva: World Health Organization.

16. Zachary, G (2001). Call them the ghost wards. *Wall Street Journal*, 24 January.

17. Martineau, T, K Decker and P Bundred (2002). Briefing note on international migration of health professionals: Leveling the playing field for developing country health systems. Liverpool: Liverpool School of Tropical Medicine.

18. Kober, K and W Van Damme (2006). Public sector nurses in Swaziland: Can the downturn be reversed? Human Resources for Health 4, (13). www.human-resources-health.com/content/4/1/13; Chikanda, A (2005). Nurse migration from Zimbabwe: Analysis of recent trends and implications. Nurse Inquiry, 12(3), pp. 162–174.

19. Buchan, J and J Sochalski (2004). Nurse migration: Trends and the policy context. Unpublished manuscript.

20. HSEA. (2003). National report: Supervised clinical placements (overseas nurses & midwives). Dublin: Health Service Employers Agency. www.hsea.ie/; HSE. (2004). National report: Adaptation placements (overseas trained nurses & midwives). Dublin: Health Service Executive. www.hsea.ie/; NMC. (2005). Statistical analysis of the register. 1 April 2004 to 31 March 2005. Report August 2005. London: Nursing and Midwifery Council. www.nmc-uk.org/aFrameDisplay.aspx?DocumentID=856

21. ICN. (2004). The global shortage of registered nurses: An overview of issues and actions. Geneva: International Council of Nurses; Department of Health and Children. (2001). The nursing and midwifery resource: Guidance for best practices on the recruitment of overseas nurses and midwives. Dublin: Nursing Policy Division Department of Health and Children. www.dohc.ie/publications/recruitment_of_overseas_nurses_and_midwives.html

22. ICN. (2005). International migration of nurses: Trends and policy implications. Geneva: International Council of Nurses.

23. Dovlo, D (2005). Commentary. Wastage in the health workforce: Some perspectives from African countries. Human Resources for Health 3(6). www.human-resources-health.com/content/3/1/6; Chikanda, A (2005). Nurse migration from Zimbabwe: Analysis of recent trends and implications. Nurse Inquiry, 12(3), pp. 162–174.

24. WHO. (2006). The world health report 2006—Working together for health. Geneva: World Health Organization.

25. Simoens, S, M Villeneuve and J Hurst (2005). Tackling nurse shortages in OECD countries. Paris: Organisation for Economic Co-operation and Development.

26. Hecker, D (2005). Occupational employment projections to 2014. *Monthly Labor Review*, 128(11), pp. 10–101.

27. Volqvartz, J (2005). The brain drain. *The Guardian*, 11 March.

28. Kingma, M (2006). Nurses on the move: Migration and the global health care economy. Ithaca: Cornell University Press.

29. PAHO. (2001). Report on technical meeting on managed migration of skilled nursing personnel. Bridgetown, Barbados: Pan American Health Organization.

30. IOM. (2003). World migration 2003: Managing migration—Challenges and responses for people on the move. Geneva: International Organization for Migration.

31. Brown, R and J Connell (2004). The migration of doctors and nurses from South Pacific Island nations. Social Science and Medicine 58, pp. 2193–2210.

32. Simoens, S, M Villeneuve and J Hurst (2005). Tackling nurse shortages in OECD countries. Paris: Organisation for Economic Co-operation and Development.

33. Padarath, A, C Chamberlain, D McCoy, A Ntuli, M Rowson and R Loewenson (2003). Health personnel in Southern Africa: Confronting misdistribution and brain drain. Equinet Discussion Paper, no. 4. Harare: Equinet. www.queensu.ca/samp/migrationresources/braindrain/documents/equinet.pdf

34. WHO. (2006). The world health report 2006—Working together for health. Geneva: World Health Organization.

35. Kingma, M (2006). Nurses on the move: Migration and the global health care economy. Ithaca: Cornell University Press.

36. ICN. (2005). International migration of nurses: Trends and policy implications. Geneva: International Council of Nurses; WHO. (2006). The world health report 2006—Working together for health. Geneva: World Health Organization.

37. Chandra, A and WK Willis (2005). Importing nurses: Combating the nursing shortage. Hospital Topics, 83(2), pp. 33–37.

38. Kingma, M (1999). Discrimination in nursing. International Nursing Review 46(3), pp. 87–90.

39. WHO. (2006). The world health report 2006—Working together for health. Geneva: World Health Organization.

40. Timur, S (2000). Changing tends and major issues in international migration: An overview of the UNESCO programmes. International Migration 165: pp. 255–269. New York, USA: Center for Migration Studies; Findlay, A and L Lowell (2002). Migration of highly skilled persons from developing countries: impact and policy responses. ILO Migration paper no 43. International Labour Office, Geneva, Switzerland.

41. IOM. (2003). World migration 2003: Managing migration—Challenges and responses for people on the move. Geneva: International Organization for Migration.

42. ICN. (2005). International migration of nurses: Trends and policy implications. Geneva: International Council of Nurses.

43. Kingma, M (2006). Nurses on the move: Migration and the global health care economy. Ithaca: Cornell University Press.

44. Troy, P, L Wyness and E McAuliffe (2007). Nurses' experiences of recruitment and migration from developing countries: a phenomenological approach. Human Resources for Health 5: p. 15.

45. Reprinted with permission from ICN (2002) Career Moves and Migration: Critical Questions. Geneva: International Council of Nurses. www.icn.ch/CareerMovesMigangl.pdf.

46. Alvez Tan, J (2006). The challenge of managing migration, retention and the return of health professionals. Academy Health power point presentation.

47. International Centre on Nurse Migration. (2007). Fact sheet: International migration and remittances. http://www.intlnursemigration.org/research.shtml.

48. Humphries, N, R Brugha and H McGee (2009). Sending money home: a mixed-methods study of remittances by migrant nurses in Ireland. Human Resources for Health 7: p. 66.

49. Ruiz, N (2008). Migration and development brief 6: Managing migration: Lessons from the Philippines. World Bank.

50. WHO. (2006). Working Together for Health. Geneva, World Health Organization.

51. Aiken, L (2004). Trends in international nurse migration. Health Affairs.

52. Ruiz, N (2008). Migration and development brief 6: Managing migration: Lessons from the Philippines. World Bank.

53. Thomas, P (2006). The international migration of Indian nurses. International nursing review 53: pp. 277–283.

54. Excerpt from a piece by MA Hodgson, The Queen's Nurses' Magazine, August 1909; http://www.districtnursing150.org.uk/stories_bermuda.htm

55. Nursing and Midwifery Council. www.nmc-uk.org. The Nursing and Midwifery Council (NMC), formerly the United Kingdom Central Council for Nursing, Midwifery and Health Visiting (UKCC), is the UK regulator for nurses, midwives and specialist community public health nurses. It maintains a register of all nurses, midwives and specialist community public health nurses eligible to work in the UK.

The Workplace: Hospital, Home and Beyond

1. Designed with Care: Design and neighbourhood healthcare buildings, London: Commission for Architecture and the Built Environment, 2006. pp. 55–57. www.cabe.org.uk

2. Burton, Adrian, Building to make people better, The Lancet, Vol 6, July 2005.

3. Allan, J, Lubetkin: Architecture and the Tradition of Progress, RIBA Publications, 1992 for an extensive piece on Finsbury Health Centre.

4. Prasad, S (ed.), Changing Hospital Architecture, RIBA Publishing, 2008.

5. Noble, A and R Dixon, St Thomas' Hospital Ward Evaluation, MARU, 1977, which compares evaluations of staff and patient's experiences of three different wards.

6. Adapted from a presentation by Dr Kirk Hamilton, President, Center for Innovation in Health Facilities in Houston, Texas, to the planning committee of the McGill University Health Centre at the Healing by Design conference, Montréal, 2000.

7. "Inquiry: Does One Size Fit All?", http://www.worldhealthdesign.com/does-one-size-fit-all.aspx.

8. Smith, HL, "It started with Florence Nightingale. 100 years later another tradition is emerging", Design, March 1966, p. 207.

9. Ulrich, R and C Zimring, The Role of the Physical Environment in the Hospital of the 21st Century: A Once-in-a-Lifetime Opportunity, a report to The Center for Health Design for the Designing

the *21st Century Hospital Project*, funded by the Robert Wood Johnson Foundation, September 2004. Evidence-based design (EBD) is defined by the Center for Health Design in California as 'the process of basing decisions about the built environment on credible research to achieve the best possible outcomes'.

10. Adapted from a presentation by Dr Roger Ulrich, Director of the Center for Health Systems and Design at Texas A&M University, to the planning committee of the McGill University Health Centre at the *Healing by Design* conference, Montréal, 2000.

11. see, for example, *The Impact of office design on business performance*, London: Commission for Architecture and the Built Environment and The British Council for Offices, 2005.

12. *Radical improvements in hospital design: Healthy Hospitals campaign report*, London: Commission for Architecture and the Built Environment, 2003.

13. *Radical improvements in hospital design: Healthy Hospitals campaign report*, London: Commission for Architecture and the Built Environment, 2003.

14. *The role of hospital design in the recruitment, retention and performance of NHS nurses in England: Executive Summary*, London: Commission for Architecture and the Built Environment, 2004.

15. *The role of hospital design in the recruitment, retention and performance of NHS nurses in England: Full Report*, PricewaterhouseCoopers LLP, in association with the University of Sheffield and Queen Margaret University College, Edinburgh for CABE, London: Commission for Architecture and the Built Environment, 2004; *The role of hospital design in the recruitment, retention and performance of NHS nurses in England: Executive Summary*, London: Commission for Architecture and the Built Environment, 2004.

16. *The role of hospital design in the recruitment, retention and performance of NHS nurses in England: Executive Summary*, London: Commission for Architecture and the Built Environment, 2004.

17. *The role of hospital design in the recruitment, retention and performance of NHS nurses in England: Full Report,* London: Commission for Architecture and the Built Environment, 2004, p. 14.

18. Queen's Nursing Institute, *2020 Vision: Focusing on the Future of Community Nursing*, London, 2009.

19. www.districtnursing150.org.uk

20. http://www.districtnursing150.org.uk/ stories_dj_gillett.htm

21. Hockey, L, *Feeling the Pulse: A Survey of District Nursing in Six Areas,* Queen's Institute of District Nursing, London, 1966.

Transforming Care

1. Kohn, L, J Corrigan and M Donaldson (eds.) Institute of Medicine (IOM), *To Err is Human: Building a Safer Health System,* The National Academies Press, Washington: 2000. http://www.nap.edu/books/0309068371/html/

2. DeWitt C and Baldwin Jr MD, Some historical notes on interdisciplinary and interprofessional education and practice in health care in the USA, *Journal of Interprofessional Care*, 2007, Vol. 21, No. s1, pp. 23–37.

3. Cherkasky, M (1949). The Montefiore Hospital home care program. *American Journal of Public Health*, 39, pp. 163–166.

4. Wise, H, The primary care team, *Archives of Internal Medicine*, 130, 1972, pp. 438–444.

5. Kohn, L, J Corrigan and M Donaldson (eds.), Institute of Medicine (IOM), *To Err is Human: Building a Safer Health System,* The National Academies Press, Washington: 2000. http://www.nap.edu/books/0309068371/html/

6. Page, A (ed.) Institute of Medicine (IOM), *Keeping Patients Safe: Transforming the Work Environment of Nurses*, The National Academies Press, Washington: 2004, Appendix B.

7. Schmitt, Madeline, in Hugh Barr, *Effective Interprofessional Education*, Blackwell Publishing Ltd: 2005; IOM Report *Keeping Patients Safe: Transforming the Work Environment of Nurses* (2004) Appendix B p. 341.

8. Madeline H Schmitt, November 2009, at the University of Virginia, *Why Interprofessional Education? Why Now?* (available on Youtube).

9. Baldwin, D (2007) *Journal of Interprofessional Care.* 21(S1): pp. 97–107.

10. *Nursing in an Evolving Health System*. Round table discussion organised by the Institute for Strategic Analysis and Innovation of the McGill University Health Centre, May 2009. www.healthinnovationforum.org.

11. Walby, Sylvia and June Greenwell with Lesley Mackay and Keith Soothill, *Medicine and Nursing—Professions in a Changing Health Service*, London: Sage, 1994, p. 2, pp. 56–60.

12. Janet McCray (ed.), *Nursing and Multi-professional Practice*, Los Angeles: Sage, 2009, pp. 25–26.

13. Kobe University Graduate School of Health Sciences, *The Reports about Educational Activities and Outcomes on Kobe University Interprofessional Education Program*, good practice grant support by Minister of Education and Science. 2007, 2008, 2009 (in Japanese).

14. Tamura Y, Y Ishikawa, P Bontje, T Shirakawa, H Andou, I Miyawaki, K Watanabe, Y Miura, R Ono, K Hirata, M Hirai and K Seki, Becoming Interprofessional at Kobe University. Chapter in: *Advanced Initiatives in Interprofessional Education in Japan* (ed. Watanabe, H), Tokyo: Springer, Japan, 2009; Kobe University Interprofessional Education Center, http://www.edu.kobe-u.ac.jp/fhs-gpipw/eng/index.html

15. Kennedy, Maureen "Shawn". *Gallup Poll: Power Elite Believes Nurses Should Have More Say in Policy, Management.* http://ajnoffthecharts.com/2010/01/25/gallup-poll-power-elite-believes-nurses-should-have-more-say-in-policy-management/

16. Wald, Lillian. *The House on Henry Street.*

17. Visiting Nurse Service of New York. http://www.vnsny.org/vnsny-research/.

18. Wald, Lillian. The Nurses' Settlement in New York. *American Journal of Nursing*, 2(8), May 1902, pp. 567–574; Henry Street Settlement. http://www.henrystreet.org/site/PageServer?pagename=abt_hssBuildings_headQuarters.

19. Rogers, Lina L, The Nurse in the Public School. *AJN*, 5(11), August 1905, pp. 764–772.

20. Wald, Lillian. The Nurses' Settlement in New York. *AJN*, 2(8), May 1902, pp. 567–574. Henry Street Settlement. http://www.henrystreet.org/site/PageServer?pagename=abt_hssBuildings_headQuarters. Linsay, Nellie C, Insurance Nursing in Rochester. *AJN*, 11(8), May 1911, pp. 614–616.

21. Henry Holt and Company, New York: 1915 pp. 38–39.

22. Frontier Nursing Service, Inc., http://www.frontiernursing.org/History/HowFNSbegan.shtm

23. Schorr and Kennedy, *100 Years of American Nursing-Celebrating a Century of Caring,* Lippincott Williams & Wilkins, New York: 1999, p.107.

24. Silver, Henry and Loretta Ford, The pediatric nurse practitioner at Colarado, *AJN*, 67(7), July 1967, pp. 1443–1444.

25. Reiter, Frances, The Nurse Clinician, *AJN*, 66(2), February 1966, pp. 274–280.

26. Bowar-Ferres, Susan, Loeb Center and Its Philosophy of Nursing, *AJN*, 75(5), May 1975, pp. 810–815.

27. Manthey, Marie, Primary Nursing Is Alive and Well in the Hospital, *AJN*, 73(1), January 1973, pp. 83–87; http://mariesnursingsalon.wordpress.com/2009/06/09/40th-anniversary-of-primary-nursing/

28. Lubic, Ruth Watson, Childbirthing Centers: Delivering More for Less, *AJN*, July 1983–Volume 83–Issue 7–ppg 1053-1056.

29. Knowlton, Leslie, Labor of Love: Nurse Midwife Ruth Watson Lubic, *AJN* 107(4), April 2007, pp. 86–87.

30. Naylor, Mary and Stacen A Keating, Transitional Care, *AJN*, 108(9), September 2008, pp. 58–63.

31. Mason, Diana J, Transitional Care (editorial), *AJN*, 109(10), October 2009, pp. 29–30.

32. Laurant, M et al, Substitution of doctors by nurses in primary care, *The Cochrane Database of Systematic Reviews* 2004, Issue 4, Art. No.: CD001271.pub2. October 2004.

33. To access all six guides, http://www.dh.gov.uk/en/Healthcare/Primarycare/TCS/TransformationalGuidescoveringsixserviceareas/DH_100223

34. http://www.rcn.org.uk/newsevents/campaigns/dignity

35. *Defending Dignity: Challenges and opportunities for nursing*, Royal College of Nursing, London, June 2008.

36. All *Dignity* material can be sourced via RCN Publications.

Picture Credits

p. 104. Dennis Gilbert.
p. 105. Keith Hunter.
p. 108. Tim Soar.
p. 109. Christopher Simon Sykes.
p. 110. Crown Copyright/Queen's Nursing Institute.
pp. 112–113. Queen's Nursing Institute.
p. 114. Queen's Nursing Institute.
p. 115. Barnet Saidman/Queen's Nursing Institute.
p. 117. Courtesy of Geoff Hunt.
p. 119. Courtesy of Krisan Palmer.
p. 120. All: Courtesy of Lois Scott.
p. 124. Zachary Nola.
p. 125. Courtesy of Carol Etherington.
p. 127. Courtesy of Carol Etherington.
p. 129. Wellcome Library, London.
p. 132. Andrya Hill.
p. 133. Courtesy of Royal College of Nursing.
pp. 134–135. Christiane Roth/Médecins Sans Frontières.
p. 136. All: Courtesy of Ghislaine Télémaque.
p. 139. All: Courtesy of Ghislaine Télémaque.
pp. 140–141. Becker Medical Library/ Washington University School of Medicine.
p. 143. Queen's Nursing Institute.
p. 144. Yumi Tamura.
p. 148. Copyright Brasiliao/Shutterstock Images LLC.
p. 151. Veronica D'souza.
p. 153. Copyright Donald Joski/Shutterstock Images LLC.
p. 155. Courtesy of Flavia Simphronio Balbino and Dr Ana Lucia Goulart, Sao Paolo Hospital.
p. 156. Yumi Tamura.
p. 158. Photograph supplied by Yuko Kuroda from the Hanshin Elderly and Disabled Support Network/Yumi Tamura.
p. 159. Yumi Tamura.
p. 162. Courtesy of Candice Pellett.
p. 164. Copyright Monkey Business Images/ Shutterstock Images LLC.
pp. 166–167. All: Design Council.
p. 169. Courtesy of International Council of Nursing.
p. 170. World Health Organization.
p. 171. Courtesy of International Council of Nursing.

pp. 172–173. Center for Disease Control and Prevention.

Back cover: World Health Organization (top right and bottom, second from left).

Thank You

All the nurses interviewed for the book: Ann Dannatt, Ann Noble, Anne Conrod Usher and the class of '59 whose stories at their last reunion were so inspirational, Anne Rook, Architects for Health, Christine Hancock, Claudia Bloom, Dennis Gilbert, Eamonn Sullivan, Fiona Bourne, Florence Nightingale Museum, particularly Caroline Worthington and Kirsteen Nixon and Elizabeth Parbutt; Harriet Coeling, International Council of Nurses, particularly Linda Carrier-Walker, Mireille Kingma and Lindsey Williamson; Jean Gray, Louise Boden, Maggie's Cancer Caring Centres, particularly Tricia Crosbie; Maureen "Shawn" Kennedy, Natalia James, Nigel Greenhill, Pamela Kelley, Queen's Nursing Institute, particularly Matthew Bradby; Ray and Viddy Moss, Ronnie Pollock, Royal College of Nursing, particularly Amanda Callaghan, Janet Davies, Jayne Buchanan; Susan McGann, Sarah Waller, Sebastian Costa, Thelma McCorquodale, the NICU nurses at the Royal Victoria Hospital, the nurses of the McGill University Health Centre, including Judith Ritchie for her early guidance, Valerie Shannon and Susan Drouin.

And thanks to the boys in our lives: Adam, Cato and James.

© 2010 Black Dog Publishing Limited, London, UK and authors.
All rights reserved.

Edited by Kate Trant and Susan Usher.

Designed by Johanna Bonnevier and Rachel Pfleger at Black Dog Publishing.

Black Dog Publishing Limited
10a Acton Street
London WC1X 9NG
United Kingdom

ISBN 978 1 906155 99 5

British Library Cataloguing-in-Publication Data. A CIP record for this book is available from the British Library.

Black Dog Publishing Limited, London, UK, is an environmentally responsible company. *NURSE past, present and future* is printed in on an FSC certified paper.

architecture art design
fashion history photography
theory and things

black dog
publishing

www.blackdogonline.com

london uk